MEET MARTIN LUTHER

MEET MARTIN LUTHER

A Sketch of the Reformer's Life

Anthony Selvaggio

Reformation Heritage Books
Grand Rapids, Michigan

Meet Martin Luther
© 2017 by Anthony Selvaggio

Reformation Heritage Books
2965 Leonard St. NE
Grand Rapids, MI 49525
616–977–0889 / Fax 616–285–3246
orders@heritagebooks.org
www.heritagebooks.org

Printed in the United States of America
17 18 19 20 21 22/10 9 8 7 6 5 4 3 2 1

Library of Congress Cataloging-in-Publication Data

Names: Selvaggio, Anthony T., author.
Title: Meet Martin Luther : a sketch of the reformer's life / Anthony Selvaggio.
Description: Grand Rapids, Michigan : Reformation Heritage Books, 2017.
Identifiers: LCCN 2016055259 (print) | LCCN 2016056508 (ebook) | ISBN 9781601785220 (pbk. : alk. paper) | ISBN 9781601785237 (epub)
Subjects: LCSH: Luther, Martin, 1483-1546. | Reformation—Germany—Biography. | Lutheran Church—Germany—Clergy—Biography.
Classification: LCC BR325 .S45 2017 (print) | LCC BR325 (ebook) | DDC 284.1092 [B]—dc23
LC record available at https://lccn.loc.gov/2016055259

For additional Reformed literature, request a free book list from Reformation Heritage Books at the above regular or e-mail address.

Contents

Chapter 1

The Young Luther

Michelangelo, Leonardo Da Vinci, Niccolo Machiavelli, Christopher Columbus. These are just a few of the transformative historical figures whose lives spanned the fifteenth and sixteenth centuries. This was the period of the Renaissance, when the continent of Europe flourished with creativity, artistic expression, exploration, and scientific discovery. It was a time that irreversibly altered the course of Western civilization. During this time there lived a man named Martin Luther (1483–1546).

Arguably, Martin Luther, and the Protestant Reformation that he set in motion, eclipses all of these other great figures and their contributions to the development of Western civilization. It is not an exaggeration to declare that he changed the world. The ripple effects of his significance continue to be felt and experienced by the Western world to this day. Even after nearly five hundred years, Martin

Luther is still relevant, particularly to every Christian who refers to himself or herself as a Protestant.

Clearly, such an influential person is worthy of study simply because of his historical and theological significance, but this is not the only reason to study the life of Luther. As with the lives of biblical figures like Hosea and Jonah, Luther's life provides us not only with historical fact but also with theological truth. It is a story of the gospel itself in that it not only presents us with dates, facts, and fascinating events but also provides us with an object lesson of faith, grace, and the forgiveness that can be found only in Jesus Christ. This is what makes Luther's life so worthy of our time and attention: it points us to Jesus and the enduring power of His death and resurrection.

The Mansfeld Years: The Son of Hans and Margaret Luder

Martin Luther was born on November 10, 1483, to Hans and Margaret Luder. Martin chose to change his surname from Luder to Luther in 1517 because the latter was etymologically related to the Greek word for "free" or "freedom." Of course, the freedom that Luther experienced in 1517 was his newly found understanding of the gospel of Jesus Christ.

On the day following Martin's birth, Hans and Margaret presented Martin for baptism. Parents did not delay baptizing their children in those times due to the high rate of infant mortality. He was baptized on the Feast of Saint Martin, and thus his parents bestowed on him the name of that patron saint.

Martin was born into a world in which life was hard. Death was ever present as plagues ravaged Europe. Most people were peasants, and very few had the privilege of education. Martin was fortunate enough to be born to parents who possessed both industry and family connections that opened the doors of educational opportunity to him.

Luther's father, Hans, was not from a noble or rich family. This meant he could not rely on inheriting wealth or land. Instead, he had to seek his own fortune in the world. He saw promise in the copper industry and thus moved his family to Mansfeld, a region of Germany known for its flourishing copper mines. Mansfeld was Martin's home during his early childhood, and he remained there until 1497.

Hans was an industrious and ambitious man. He labored in the copper mines for seven years, eventually purchasing his own mine. He subsequently acquired additional mines, gradually working his way up to an upper middle-class existence and becoming a respected member of his community. He even served as a member of the Mansfeld city council. Although Hans worked his way up the socioeconomic ladder, he did have some help as he climbed. That help came from his capable and connected wife, Margaret.

Margaret Luder, affectionately referred to as Hanna by her family, did not come from peasant stock; rather, her family was both educated and socially connected. She was a part of the Lindemann family, a well-established and well-regarded family from Eisenach. The Lindemanns were committed to education, and, as we shall see, they played a significant role in Martin's own education. They would not only help Martin navigate the world of higher education but would also help Hans establish himself in the copper industry. Hans required capital to purchase his mines, which he obtained through loans. It is likely that the Lindemanns assisted him in securing this credit. It seems clear that Hans's success was partially linked to Margaret's family.

Martin's mother was a stern and dutiful woman. As the Luder family had no servants during Martin's childhood years, his mother's days were filled with domestic labor and the responsibilities of rearing and disciplining young children. At times, his mother exacted rather severe punishment on Martin for his transgressions. One time he was caught in the act of stealing a nut, and his mother struck him so forcefully that she drew blood. Martin never forgot that incident. Her role in his life has sometimes been neglected, with historians tending to focus solely on the influence of his father, but that would render an incomplete picture of Luther. His mother loomed large in his life. Her social background and family connections, as well as her stern discipline, served as catalysts for the man that Luther would become.

Interestingly, Martin's mother would also become a target for the slander perpetrated by his enemies. One of the more wicked acts of slander against his mother was that his birth was the result of her having bathhouse relations with the devil.

These charges persisted throughout Martin's life, and he once remarked regarding their futility,

> If the Devil can do nothing against the teachings, he attacks the person, lying slandering cursing, and ranting at him. Just as the papists' Beelzebub did to me when he could not subdue my Gospel, he wrote that I was possessed by the Devil, was a changeling, my beloved mother a whore and a bath attendant.[1]

Both Hans and Margaret Luder desired to see that Martin was educated. During his years in Mansfeld, he attended school there. It is likely that he received rather strict instruction from his teachers as they schooled him in the basics of Latin, logic, rhetoric, and grammar. From the accounts of this period of Martin's life, he apparently did not stand out as an exceptional student. His own reflections from this period display his disdain for the often arbitrary application of corporal punishment meted out by the teachers.

---

1. As quoted in Heiko A. Oberman, *Luther: Man between God and the Devil* (New Haven, Conn.: Yale University Press, 2006), 88.

Martin's early years in Mansfeld represent the foundation for the remainder of his life. He had the benefit of being born to upwardly mobile parents who valued education and were willing to sacrifice to see him benefit from such education. His mother also connected him to a level of nobility and educational access that was available to very few in his time. As we shall see, these connections would prove key to the educational advancement that equipped Martin to be a scholar, theologian, and future leader of the Reformation.

Luther Prepares for University:
Magdeburg and Eisenach

In 1497, at the age of thirteen, Martin left Mansfeld to pursue additional education. His first destination was Magdeburg, where he continued his education for one year. At Magdeburg he was placed in the custody of the Brethren of Common Life, a lay religious group created by a Dutch-inspired reform movement. The Brethren did not operate a school but rather provided lodging, oversight, and guidance to boys attending school away from home. The goal of the Brethren of Common Life was to reinforce the nexus between learning and piety, with an emphasis on the former serving the latter. They stressed a life of simple piety rather than the strict system of vows that governed life in many monastic communities of the time. There was an element of anticlericalism in the history of the Brethren of Common Life: this resulted in the Brethren coming under scrutiny from official church orders like the Dominicans, who once accused the Brethren of heresy. At one time historians placed great weight on the Brethren's influence on Luther, claiming that the seeds of his revolt against Roman Catholicism were sown in the anticlerical soil of his time with them in Magdeburg. Recent scholarship, however, suggests that their influence on Luther has likely been overstated, particularly given that Luther was with them for only one year.

Luther took the next step in his education in 1498 when he moved to Eisenach. In his three years studying there, he began to blossom as a student. This was a time of intellectual awakening for Luther because it was there he encountered Wiegand Geldennupf, a teacher who sparked Luther's intellectual curiosity. Up until this point, Luther's educational experiences were far from favorable, and his recollection of them primarily focused on the harshness of his teachers and the beatings he had received. He even used the word "torture" to describe those early educational experiences. That changed at Eisenach as the rote memorization drills that dominated his early education gave way to creative and critical thinking. Here, Luther was exposed to great classical authors like Virgil and to great works like *Aesop's Fables*. Luther learned both effective oration and persuasive writing skills. This was a happy time in Luther's life, and he later recounted it with fondness.

His years at Eisenach were influential for reasons beyond the quality of his formal education experienced there. In Eisenach, Luther had the privilege of being taken into the home of Heinrich Schalbe, an influential man who eventually became mayor of Eisenach. It appears that the Schalbe family had connections to the Luders, likely through his mother's side of the family in particular. In the Schalbe home he had the privilege of participating in what Luther described as the "Schalbense Collegium," a moniker he bestowed because of the climate of intellectual and pious conversation he experienced there.

Luther also made another dear friend in Eisenach—Johannes Braun, the vicar at the Church of Saint Mary. Although significantly older than Luther, he served as a friend as well as a role model. Even after Luther moved on from Eisenach he maintained correspondence with Braun in which he revealed his warmth and affection for his mentor. He once described Braun as his very closest friend. As we shall see, Luther was a man who cultivated and relied on close personal friendships marked by loyalty, intimacy, and trust. During his life he had some deep friendships that exerted a great deal of influence on him.

As Luther neared the end of his three-year program of study at Eisenach, his teacher Wiegand Geldennupf and the school's wise headmaster, John Trebonius, recognized that Luther had the intellectual gifts to pursue further education at university. It was uncommon for a young man from Luther's social strata to attend university at this time, and it would have been a significant commitment and sacrifice for his family, but Luther's father approved of him pursuing additional studies at university. It is likely, once again, that the influence of his mother and her well-educated family was a major contributing factor in Luther's ability to continue to pursue his education.

A Scholar Is Born: The Years at Erfurt

The next stop in Luther's academic journey was the University of Erfurt. The city of Erfurt was a place of commerce surrounded by fortified walls, which gave its inhabitants a sense of security and safety. It was also a place of significant religious activity, with one thousand of its twenty thousand inhabitants being part of some religious order. In fact, Erfurt was so well known for its religious emphasis it was often referred to as "little Rome." It was within the city's fortified walls that young Martin would come of age as a scholar.

Luther entered the University of Erfurt in 1501. The university was the third largest in Germany and had a sound reputation. His choice to study there likely reflects the influence of his mother and her family. Many members of the Lindemann family had chosen to study at Erfurt, and it is likely that his mother and her family prodded Luther in this direction.

Luther earned his bachelor of arts degree in just one year, completing it in September of 1502.

He completed his master of arts degree three years later in January of 1505. During his time at Erfurt, Luther was subjected to a rigorous course of studies, and his life was extremely regulated. Here he was exposed to the thought of Aristotle, whose works served as the core scholarly authority for most European universities. Perhaps one of the most lasting features of his education at Erfurt was the two years Luther spent debating various aspects of Aristotle's thought. These debates required students to use logic and rhetoric in a public setting to advance their respective positions. It was here that Luther learned to handle himself in contentious public disputations and to refine his persuasive writing skills. These two skills, public debate and persuasive writing, would serve Luther well in the future as he entered the intense debates during the Reformation.

When Luther began his studies at Erfurt he was not among the top of his class, but he worked extremely hard and quickly rose through the ranks of the student body. This was a pleasant and enjoyable time for Luther. He generally liked his classes and instructors. The University of Erfurt was a verdant intellectual environment that exposed

Luther to the innovative scholarly and philosophical debates of his day. By the time he completed his master of arts in 1505, Luther was a well-trained academic.

Luther recounted attaining his master's degree as one of the most splendid events in his life. He reveled in the ceremonies surrounding his accomplishment. This was a tremendous achievement, particularly given the relatively modest socio-economic status of his family. His father began referring to him as "Master Martin" with fatherly pride. It was expected that a student who had completed his master's would next pursue one of the three prominent professional courses of study—law, medicine, or theology. It was clear which course his father preferred—Hans Luder wanted his son to be a lawyer. Luther initially followed his father's wishes for his life and enrolled to study the law, but the course of his studies and life would soon take a very different direction. Luther had experienced great academic success, but he was also about to experience the first major crisis of his life.

Chapter 2
The Crisis and the Cowl

In 1505, Luther was twenty-two years old and the bearer of a master's degree from one of the most prestigious universities in Germany. He had honored his mother by following in the footsteps of many of her family members in attending the University of Erfurt and had also pleased his father by distinguishing himself as a scholar and by choosing to further his studies in the area of jurisprudence. In fact, his father was so overjoyed with Luther's choice to pursue the law as a career that he purchased, at great expense, a copy of Corpus Juris Civilis (the legal code of Roman emperor Justinian), which was the leading legal text at this time. Luther had come of age and had fulfilled the hopes and dreams of his parents. He was destined to have a lucrative legal career in the service of some nobleman or as part of the nascent German bureaucracy. But the path of his life took an abrupt turn in the summer of 1505.

The Storm at Stotternheim

On July 2, 1505, as Luther was traveling to visit his parents, the skies began to grow ominous. As he neared the village of Stotternheim, he found himself in the midst of a severe thunderstorm, and a particularly violent lightning strike sent him to the ground in fear. In the midst of his terror he cried out to Saint Anne and made his now famous vow, "Help me, Saint Anne, I will become a monk!"

The importance of this moment for Luther cannot be overestimated. Over the course of his life he would make frequent reference to this life-changing experience. It was an event that he would often reinterpret and reflect on. At times he even chastised himself for being superstitious regarding its meaning, but he never failed to admit that the Lord had used this event to change his life. Historians have debated the significance of this incident, disagreeing as to whether it immediately changed Luther's course of life or whether it was simply a catalyst that furthered his heart toward a choice he was already inclined to make. Either way, that lightning strike may well be considered one of the most important events in the course of history, for it contributed to Luther exchanging his law books for a cowl. Master Martin was headed for the monastery.

Martin wrote to his father to explain what had occurred on his trip home and the vow he had made in the midst of the storm. He told of his plan to keep this vow and enter the monastery. Not surprisingly, his father did not take this news well. In fact, Hans Luder was irate over his son's rash decision making. He questioned Luther regarding his interpretation of these events, intimating that he may be misguided in his conclusions. Hans believed his son was about to waste his costly education. Luther was not shaken or moved by his father's initial hostility to his decision to keep his vow. His friends also thought he had lost his senses, and they too attempted to change his mind, but Luther remained unmoved.

Luther began making preparations to enter the monastic life. He returned the costly legal books his father had purchased for him, as he knew he could take nothing with him into this new life. He then invited his friends to a farewell dinner. It was very much like a last supper for Luther. Entering the monastic life meant that you set the secular world aside—your worldly relationships and goods must be left at the monastery door. So Luther gathered his friends together on the evening of July 16, a mere two weeks after making his vow, and said good-bye to them. The next morning, July 17, 1505, those same friends followed Luther to the door of an Augustinian monastery in Erfurt where he reportedly told them, "You see me today and never again."

Entering the Black Cloister

The events that brought Luther to the monastic life are rife with humorous ironies and acts of extraordinary providence. For instance, there is the irony that the Protestant Reformation can be traced back to a prayer to a canonized saint and a vow to become a Roman Catholic monk. Then there was Luther's choice of religious order. Here is where we see the great hand of Providence. Erfurt offered a variety of choices for Luther when it came to the monastic life. After all, it was known as "little Rome." He could have chosen to be a Dominican, Franciscan, or Benedictine monk, but he did not. Luther chose the Augustinian order, and this choice would have profound ramifications on his life and the course of Western history. Finally, there is the profound irony that the man who would eventually change the course of the world and become a renowned public figure had, at this time, determined to cut himself off from the world by choosing to live a solitary, private, and isolated life in a monastery nestled in the walled city of Erfurt.

Why did Luther choose the Augustinian monastic order? Historians are not exactly sure, but it may have been that the Augustinians emphasized scholarship, which appealed very much to Luther. He certainly did not choose an easy monastic order. Augustinian life was strictly programmed and regimented. The novices, monks in training, were subjected to wearing uncomfortable clothing, received meager nourishment, and engaged in hard labor in an effort to help them achieve the denial of worldly pleasures and the temptations of the flesh. Luther would spend a year in probation as a novice, during which he experienced all the rigors of his newly chosen life. Although he would later criticize the type of piety he practiced in the monastery, he was a model novice and applied himself faithfully to his calling. He would later note that if this time of piety could have secured a man salvation, then he would have earned such a reward by his exacting attention to detail. Luther was a model monk.

The Model Monk Celebrates His First Mass

Luther persevered through his time as a novice and, just as in his academic career, he carried himself with distinction. After a little over one year, on April 4, 1507, Luther was ordained as a priest. This was a very important achievement. In Luther's time, monks were highly regarded in their communities for their holiness and religious importance, but a monk who was also a priest entered an entirely different echelon. This is because a priest could do something a monk could never do—administer the sacrament of Holy Communion.

For most Protestant Christians today, partaking in the Lord's Supper is a relatively common phenomenon in religious life and, perhaps, has become something that Christians take for granted. Most Protestants view the Lord's Supper as a celebration involving symbols of Jesus's broken body (the bread) and shed blood (the wine). For Luther, the sacrament of Holy Communion was a profound event. As a newly ordained priest, Luther would now be able to speak the Latin words *hoc est corpus meum* (this is My body) and *hoc poculum est novem testamentum sanguinis mei* (this cup is the new testament in My blood). For Luther, speaking those words meant that the bread and wine were transformed into the actual body and blood of Jesus. One cannot overestimate the significance of the sacrament of Communion during this period of Luther's life and of church history. The celebration of Communion was referred to as the Mass, and to participate in a Mass was itself viewed as a meritorious work contributing to salvation. To participate in the Mass was a good work, but to officiate over it was like entering into the courts of heaven.

After his ordination to the priesthood, Luther was told that he would officiate his first Mass on May 2, 1507. He feverishly studied the textbooks, which set forth the exact procedure of the rite and how a priest should properly conduct himself. As he labored to memorize the words and motions of the rite, he began to feel a great sense of unworthiness to administer and ingest such a holy meal. Luther was gripped with fear and dread.

In addition to his unease regarding his worthiness to conduct the rite, Luther was also filled with trepidation because his father was coming to witness his son's first formal act as a priest. Hans Luder arrived at Martin's first Mass with an entourage of twenty family members and a gift of twenty guldens for the monastery.

As Luther officiated his first Mass on that day, he was well aware of his father's presence, but he was even more anxious over the reality that he would be in the presence of his heavenly Father. During the Mass, Luther struggled with his anxiety and reported afterward that he nearly dropped the bread and the cup. He later noted that he nearly ran away at the time of speaking the words of the eucharistic prayer. But the shaken Luther persevered through the Mass and completed it with his dignity intact.

There was a banquet held in celebration of Luther's Mass, and his father attended along with the guests he brought with him. Sadly, the fractures in Luther's relationship with his father had not fully healed, and the two exchanged hurtful words. His father questioned him again regarding his interpretation of the thunderstorm and his subsequent vow, noting the possibility that the devil may have sent that storm. He also lectured his newly ordained son on the commandment to honor his father and mother, intimating that he had failed to do so by deviating from his legal studies. While we are uncertain how Luther responded to his father's barbs on that day, we do know that Luther was not shaken from his course. He was more committed than ever to pursue the path of a priest and to dedicate his life to God.

Luther's Second Father

Luther continued to excel as a monk and began to get noticed by those in authority over him. One of his superiors, Vicar General Johann von Staupitz, took particular interest in Luther. Staupitz was an influential and godly man. He had a direct line to Frederick the Wise of Saxony, who ruled over the local region and was among the seven princes who had power to elect the Holy Roman emperor. Staupitz was directly responsible for advancing Luther's career and prominence; he would also become to Luther both a father figure and friend.

In the winter of 1508, Staupitz afforded Luther an incredible opportunity for a man of his age and experience. He commissioned Martin to be a substitute professor of moral philosophy at the University of Wittenberg. Wittenberg was at this time not the most glamorous of academic assignments. It was a young, fledgling university located in what was then a remote and unsophisticated part of Germany. Luther referred to it as being almost barbaric in nature. It was a sparsely inhabited place known mainly for the brewing of strong beer, which reportedly was well consumed by its inhabitants. The school there was also not very well regarded from an academic perspective. Both Staupitz and Frederick the Wise wanted to change that, and Luther was viewed as a way to improve the faculty. While not a glamorous assignment, his temporary post at Wittenberg was the beginning of a path that would culminate in Luther eventually becoming an instructor and doctor of theology.

The next step in Luther's academic career, again prompted by Staupitz, occurred on March 9, 1509, when Luther formally began his path to a doctorate by being "admitted to the Bible." This was an incredible blessing to Luther. He had tired of studying and teaching philosophy and longed to dedicate himself to the study of Scripture. Luther was on his way to his doctorate.

The importance of Luther's relationship with Staupitz is difficult to exaggerate. Luther had essentially lost his relationship with his biological father over his decision to pursue theology rather than law as a vocation. In Staupitz, Luther found a new father. He was a wise, learned, older, and—most importantly—godly man who took a keen interest in Luther's life and shared his priorities. Their relationship became so close that many of Luther's peers were jealous of it and even believed Luther was the beneficiary of favoritism. It is true that Staupitz provided Luther with opportunities that were beyond his years and experience, but Luther was also an excellent and gifted monk. It is difficult to know how much of his success was attributed to merit versus Staupitz's affection for him. It was likely a mixture of these realities that propelled Luther's career forward at such a rapid pace.

The significance of Staupitz in Luther's life was not limited merely to academic promotions. Staupitz also became a spiritual father to Luther. In fact, he became the man to whom Luther confessed his sins, which Luther became obsessed with. For the monks of the cloister, confession was extremely rigorous and easily led to great despair. The lives of the monks were so regulated that they could hardly have committed a gross sin even if they so desired. This meant that the monk in confession began to fixate on his inner motives rather than outward actions. The confessor would probe the confessing monk's innermost thoughts in an effort to find any seedling of sin in his soul. Luther, like many of his fellow monks, found this a torturous affair. Such introspective soul-searching led many monks into depression. They even developed a term for the feelings this type of confession produced in them—*in cloaca*, which meant something like "down in the dumps." Luther experienced these feelings with ever greater acuteness. Some of his confessional sessions lasted as long as six hours. In fact, he became so obsessed with confessing every impure thought and motive that Staupitz had to frequently chastise him and bring him back to reality. At one point Staupitz chided Luther by observing that he would confess every act of flatulence! Luther would later note the significance of his mentor in keeping him from falling into the abyss of despair.

Luther had entered a phase of his life when he began to feel crippled with doubt and ridden by anxiety. It is not that he began to doubt God's existence but that he began to struggle with how he could ever possibly know assurance of his salvation. He was looking for certainty of the truth of God's forgiveness but was becoming less certain of the authority of the church and its teachings. He began to doubt the efficacy of all that he was doing as a monk. He was nearing a second crisis in his life. Then, in November of 1510, his second father came to him and gave him a new assignment. Staupitz enlisted Luther to go to Rome, the holy city, to broker a dispute among factions of feuding monks. This was a dream come true for Luther. He was afforded an opportunity to travel to the heart of Christendom, a place he then believed to be among the holiest locations on earth. Luther eagerly prepared for his journey to Rome.

Luther Goes to Rome
Luther had great expectations regarding his trip to Rome. There he would have opportunity to celebrate Mass and see the holy relics of Christendom, such as the bones of the apostles Peter and Paul.

Rome also offered many ways to perform meritorious works that could be applied to free loved ones from purgatory. As Luther departed for Rome he was stirred with excitement, but that excitement would quickly dwindle.

Getting to Rome was itself a taxing and arduous process. Luther made the trip on foot. His long and exhausting journey took him through the rough terrain of the Alps. When Luther finally arrived, he beheld the holy city and was initially struck by its glory, but as he entered he became utterly disgusted by its decadence.

On the streets of Rome Luther witnessed rampant prostitution and generally unsanitary conditions. Citizens frequently urinated in public and simply tossed the contents of their chamber pots into the public streets. He saw little holy about this city.

Luther's hopes for his trip to Rome were further deflated by his experiences in the churches and with the clergy there. He had looked forward to performing Masses in the historic and sacred churches of Rome, only to find that the local priests were corrupt and frequently rushed him through his work, even mocking Luther's piety. He was utterly crushed by what he saw and experienced in the churches there.

The doubts and struggles that Luther had been feeling prior to his trip to Rome were only exacerbated by what he experienced there. At one point he decided to scale the steps of the Santa Scala on his knees. The Santa Scala were believed to be the very steps of the palace of Pontius Pilate that had been transferred from Jerusalem to Rome. These were the steps that Christ Himself had climbed. By climbing the steps on his hands and knees, Luther believed he could free his deceased loved ones from purgatory. On each step he prayed the Lord's Prayer. He took to this task with his usual determination and soberness, but after arriving at the top of the stairs he experienced a deepening sense of skepticism and doubt. Again, this was not a doubt about his belief in God but rather a doubt about the value of things like the holy relics and the scaling of the Santa Scala. His skepticism was focused on the teachings of the church. At the top of the stairs, Luther pondered, "Who knows whether this is really true?"

Overall, Luther's trip to Rome was a disappointment to him. The city was filled with chaos, ungodliness, and filth. The clergy was blasphemous. The holy relics seemed like powerless trinkets. But this trip to Rome was not without value. In many ways, the question that Luther asked himself at the top of the Santa Scala—"Who knows whether this is really true?"—served as the beginning point of his search for a source of certainty regarding how we relate to God. It was the moment he began to question the teachings of the church and the current system. Luther was looking for a place to stand. He was seeking truth. He desired an authority he could trust. It was this inner ache for certainty, truth, and authority that led him inexorably to the Holy Scriptures. Luther's son Paul would later note that his father spoke of that moment at the top of the Santa Scala as the time when he was struck in a powerful way by these words of the apostle Paul in his epistle to the Romans—"the just shall live by faith." In this sense, Luther's pilgrimage to Rome was a major contributing factor to the birth of the Reformation.

The Way to Wittenberg

After the winter of 1510, Luther returned to Erfurt, arriving in April of 1511. He reported that his mission to resolve the dispute among the Augustinians there was not successful. Luther felt the weight of his failure and his mounting skepticism. He was twenty-six years old at this time. Then in October of 1512 Luther received a joyous surprise that would ultimately pave the way for the onset of the Reformation. His trusted mentor and spiritual father, Staupitz, informed him that he would be receiving his doctorate and would be sent to train the monks in Wittenberg. He was then told that his specific concentration would be teaching theology and preaching. Although he initially had some doubts about this calling, he quickly came to embrace it. What specifically appealed to him about this assignment was that he would be able to study the Scriptures rather than Aristotle. In mid-October of 1512, Luther received his doctor of theology and made his way to Wittenberg to teach the Bible.

Chapter 3
Wittenberg and the Word of God

Wittenberg was now Luther's home. It was not much of a town. It had none of the glories of Rome and paled in comparison to Erfurt as well. He had encountered Wittenberg before, teaching there on a temporary basis in 1508, so he was not surprised by what he saw. Luther knew this was a rugged, sparsely populated, and unsophisticated frontier town, but it had two things going for it. First, it had the young university, which was still in the process of being built when Luther arrived. Second, it had the patronage of Frederick the Wise of Saxony. Frederick desired to see the University at Wittenberg prosper, and he put his resources behind it. One of those resources was Dr. Martin Luther.

Luther took his vows committing himself to uphold the doctrine of the church, and he immediately threw himself into his work, approaching his new calling with the same indefatigable commitment with which he approached his life as a monk. He exhausted himself in preparing for his lectures. He mastered Greek and Hebrew so that he could be a more effective teacher. He gave his all and nearly collapsed under the physical and mental strain of his new assignment.

Luther's First Lectures

Luther began his formal lectures in 1513, focusing on the Psalms. After lecturing on the Psalms, he entered into the letters of Paul. In 1515, he began his lectures on Romans and followed this with lectures on Galatians in 1516–1517. One of the benefits of being in Wittenberg was that the town was home to a new invention that was quite useful to the university—the printing press. This allowed Luther to utilize specially made manuscripts for his lectures. These included the text of the Scripture passage on which he was lecturing along with wide margins in which he could write his notes on the passage.

As Luther was mining the depths of God's Word, he began to feel the awful weight of God's judgment. He was again entering into a time of depression and brutal self-evaluation. He began to see God as a condemning judge who demanded exacting righteousness from him, something Luther knew he could not provide. He even began to despise the concept of the righteousness of God, a concept he encountered frequently in his studies in Romans and Galatians. Luther was haunted by the specter of the justice of God.

Luther was a man whose life was marked by internal crises. He experienced the first in 1505 in the midst of the thunderstorm outside the village of Stotternheim when he made his vow to become a monk. Another occurred when he struggled to be the best monk and burdened Staupitz with his endless confessions. His trip to Rome represented a moment of crisis as he became disillusioned by the powerless relics and the apathetic clergy he found there. Now, Luther was experiencing yet another personal crisis as he confronted God's Word each day. He could not grasp how he would ever be found acceptable to God given His standard of justice. But unlike his previous crises, this one occurred as Luther was studying the Scriptures, and it was through that study that Luther found an answer to the questions that plagued him. In the

Scriptures, Luther found a place to stand. He found certainty. He found deliverance.

The Justice of God and the Letter to the Romans
Luther's main struggle centered on understanding God's justice. When he began his lectures on Romans, he understood God's justice to be primarily applied in meting out punishment on the unjust. This troubled Luther greatly, because although he endeavored to be holy in his life he knew he always fell short of God's exacting standards of justice. This led him to see God as one who heaps continual condemnation on us. Luther expressed this angst in the following terms:

> As if indeed it is not enough that miserable sinners, eternally lost through eternal sin, are crushed by every kind of calamity by the law of the Ten Commandments, without having God add pain to pain by the gospel and also by the gospel's threatening us with his righteousness and wrath![1]

---

1. As quoted in James M. Kittelson, *Luther the Reformer: The Story of the Man and His Career* (Minneapolis: Fortress Press, 2003), 88.

For Luther, God's justice was something to fear and resent. These feelings fomented in Luther's heart and actually resulted in his experiencing and expressing a level of anger and hatred toward God. As Luther was pondering the epistle of Paul to the Romans, he came across the phrase "the just shall live by faith" (Rom. 1:17). He reported that he spent night and day thinking on that phrase and its connection with the justice of God. He then had an epiphany that transformed his conception of God's justice. It dawned on Luther that God's justice is upheld and fulfilled when *He* justifies His people through faith. He later described the impact of this realization:

> Thereupon I felt myself to be reborn and to have gone through open doors into paradise. The whole of Scripture took on a new meaning, and whereas before the "justice of God" had filled me with hate, now it became to me inexpressibly sweet in greater love.[2]

---

2. As quoted in Roland H. Bainton, *Here I Stand: A Life of Martin Luther* (repr., London: Forgotten Books, 2012), 65.

Luther now understood God's justice as a gift—a gift made possible by Jesus Christ and His gospel. Luther recognized that Jesus was both just and the justifier. He became convinced that God provided His people, through the gift of faith, with something he called "passive justice." Passive justice is God providing for us what He commands of us. Luther came to the realization that righteousness is not something we earn through meritorious efforts; rather, it is a gift given to the believer through faith just as Paul declared it in Romans 1:17—"the just shall live by faith."

When Luther grasped this truth taught by the Scriptures, it revolutionized his life. His burdened and weary conscience was freed from its bondage. His mind was liberated from the torture of continually contemplating God's judgment on him for every sinful thought and deed in his life. He now began to turn his focus to the mercy of God provided through the person and work of Jesus Christ. He turned from focusing inside himself for an answer and instead fixed his eyes on the cross. He understood that on the cross the justice and mercy of God were perfectly satisfied in the death of Jesus Christ. Luther had truly experienced a personal revolution, but, unbeknownst to him, he was about to spark a revolution that would change the course of history.

From the Tower to the Pulpit

Luther's great breakthrough regarding his understanding of the justice of God and the meaning of Paul's phrase "the just shall live by faith" is often referred to as his "tower experience," because he realized these truths in his study, which was housed in a tower of the monastery at Wittenberg. Most historians agree that it is best to understand his "tower experience" as an evolutionary process in which he gradually grasped these principles rather than seeing it as occurring at one moment in time. But while Luther may have discovered these truths in his tower, he certainly had no intention of isolating them there. His progressive embracing of these new truths began to trickle out in the classroom and, even more profoundly and importantly, in the pulpit.

Luther's many duties at Wittenberg included preaching at the local parish. Like all of his callings, the care of his flock was a serious matter to Luther. He recognized that his struggles regarding

how a person may be justified before a holy God
were not merely personal; rather, his struggle was
shared by the people in his parish. Like Luther, the
people in his parish had been instructed to strive
for justification by means of an external system
administered under the authority of the church.
This external system focused on participating in
the sacraments of the church, performing meritorious deeds, trusting in the power of holy relics,
and purchasing indulgences.

Indulgences, according to the teachings of the
church, allowed people to receive a reprieve for the
punishment of their sins. According to the church,
if you sinned during your life you would be punished after death by being held in purgatory for a
period of time. Indulgences allowed you to shorten
or potentially eliminate your sentence in purgatory.
They could also be used to shorten the sentences
of your deceased loved ones. This had a powerful
sway over the people: a living person could continue to buy indulgences or atone for sin by means
of a pilgrimage like Luther had attempted in Rome,
but for a dead loved one an indulgence obtained by
a living relation on his or her behalf was the only
way to receive a reduced sentence.

For a sin to be indulged, the person seeking the indulgence would need to demonstrate evidence of his or her sincerity; this was most often achieved by making a financial contribution to the church. Initially, there was a separation between the granting of an indulgence and the act of financial contribution, but over time the lines were blurred and the practice became a crass financial exchange. One of the churches authorized to sell indulgences was Luther's parish at the Castle Church at Wittenberg.

His parish also began to accumulate a large collection of relics. Frederick the Wise of Saxony had committed his own personal treasure to the task of making Wittenberg a center for holy relics. One inventory, dating from 1509, listed the collection at over five thousand relics. Another inventory, dating from 1520, displays that the collection at Wittenberg had swelled to nearly twenty thousand relics. Among this vast collection was everything from a tooth of Saint Jerome to gold from one of the wise men who visited Jesus at His birth.

The selling of indulgences and the collection of holy relics were linked together in Wittenberg. Luther's flock was told that if they viewed these relics on a designated day and made a corresponding contribution to the church, they could receive indulgences that would, if the contribution was significant enough, provide for reductions in purgatorial sentences for a period up to nearly two million years.

Luther's pastoral instincts and passions were ignited by these abuses, and he slowly began to publicly speak out against indulgences. His sermons from the year 1516 reveal several measured, critical references to indulgences. Luther was still reserved and cautious at this point. He did not condemn the use of indulgences but rather stressed their dangers and suggested they could lead people into complacency regarding true confession to God. He did, however, begin to question the pope's power to deliver souls from purgatory. Luther's personal "discovery" in the tower was beginning to manifest itself in the public pulpit at Wittenberg. The sparks of these early criticisms of indulgences would soon ignite into a conflagration that would ultimately pit Luther against the pope. The catalyst for this conflagration was a peddler of indulgences named Johann Tetzel.

Johann Tetzel and Pope Leo's Indulgence

In the early part of the sixteenth century, Pope Leo X became concerned about the dismal financial condition of the papacy and its diminishing political power throughout Europe. He also very much wanted to remodel Saint Peter's Basilica, which had fallen into disrepair and which paled in comparison to the lush royal courts of Europe. Pope Leo desired to elevate his court to the level of princes and monarchs, whom he saw as his peers if not his inferiors. The problem Pope Leo faced in accomplishing this goal was that he lacked the requisite funds. Pope Leo turned his attention to the selling of indulgences as a means of raising revenues and, in the autumn of 1517, he enlisted the services of Johann Tetzel to be his chief promoter.

Tetzel was not a physically impressive man. He was short, stocky, and rather diminutive in his overall appearance. But he had one particular skill that caught the eye of the pope—he was very accomplished at selling indulgences. Tetzel was a salesman through and through, and he was excellent at his vocation.

Pope Leo recognized that in order for his newly minted indulgence to raise the needed revenue it must have some sort of cachet to it, something that the people would very much desire to buy. He decided to make this new indulgence a "plenary indulgence," which meant that it would entirely eliminate the purgatorial sentence of a person. By purchasing this type of indulgence a living person would eliminate the need to spend any time in purgatory. Also, a person could purchase this indulgence for a deceased loved one and immediately free them from the remainder of their time in purgatory. Pope Leo's new indulgence was very attractive, and Tetzel was just the man to market it to the masses of Europe.

He took to his assignment with great vigor and showmanship. When he came to town he came as a spectacle. He had a procession of horsemen with him and was bearing the coat of arms of Pope Leo's family. Trumpeters would announce his arrival and the people would gather to witness the display and hear his pitch. Tetzel tugged at the hearts of the people, particularly regarding the status of their deceased loved ones. Although meek in stature, he was quite confident and persuasive in speech. He would end his presentation by declaring, "As soon as a coin in the coffer rings, a soul from purgatory springs." The money began to flow into the coffers of the papacy. Tetzel was proving quite successful. But, unbeknownst to Tetzel, he was about to meet some resistance, which occurred the day he neared the vicinity of Wittenberg, the home of Martin Luther.

Chapter 4

The Dawn of the Reformation

Tetzel's arrival near Wittenberg was not something that Frederick the Wise welcomed. Although a proponent of relics and indulgences, Frederick did not like the idea of the pope peddling his special indulgence in areas under his care. He did not like his people being fleeced to increase the wealth of the papacy. Martin Luther also opposed Tetzel and the pope's new indulgence, but for entirely different reasons. He was not concerned about who received the money from the indulgence; rather, he was concerned about the welfare of his people and the theological deception involved in marketing this type of indulgence. Luther expressed his concerns in a powerful way—the Ninety-Five Theses.

The Ninety-Five Theses

On October 31, 1517, Martin Luther went public with his protest against abuses related to the selling of indulgences. He did this by nailing a document containing his Ninety-Five Theses to the door of the Castle Church in Wittenberg. When he did this, Tetzel was in the nearby town of Elbe selling his wares. Luther's original intended audience was the church and academy. His Ninety-Five Theses, after all, were written in Latin, a language that only educated men could understand. His intent was to spark a lively theological and academic debate among the clergy and professors. There was a custom in the university at Wittenberg whereby professors who desired an academic disputation would post the subject of the disputation on the door of the Castle Church. Thus, Luther anticipated that his audience would be a small group, but that soon changed. Luther's Ninety-Five Theses were quickly translated into German, and with the aid of the newly invented printing press, copies soon made their way throughout Germany.

It is extraordinary to think of the ramifications and ripples of that one event. This single act, by an overworked and irritated monk, was the spark that would soon set the world ablaze. Luther's act on that fateful day soon made him the adversary of incredibly powerful men and institutions, subjecting him to great personal peril. Why did he do it? Did he desire fame? Was he looking to pick a fight with Rome? Many historians have attempted to perform psychoanalysis on Luther's decision that day, but perhaps the simplest and most accurate understanding of his motivation was that he feared the Lord and loved his flock. He was simply appalled by Tetzel's methods and the way the pope had perverted the practice of selling indulgences. Luther wasn't seeking fame or a fight with Rome; he was seeking to glorify God and protect his people. His motivations were those of a faithful pastor.

The Ninety-Five Theses reflect the reality that Luther's main concern with indulgences was that they undermined the biblical doctrine of true repentance. In fact, the very first of the Ninety-Five Theses focuses on Christ's command to repent:

> When our Lord and Master Jesus Christ said, "Repent" (Mt 4:17), he willed the entire life of believers to be one of repentance.

Luther was also concerned that indulgences encouraged people to place their trust in a piece of paper rather than in the person and work of Christ.

We can see Luther's directing the believer to Christ as the source of blessing and salvation in thesis 37:

> Every true Christian, whether living or dead, has part in all the blessings of Christ and the Church; and this is granted him by God, even without letters of pardon.

In thesis 52, we witness Luther explicitly denouncing any power in the indulgence to achieve salvation:

> The assurance of salvation by letters of pardon is vain, even though the commissary, nay, even though the pope himself, were to stake his soul upon it.

In Luther's mind, indulgences were a false cure for a real problem, and he believed marketers like Tetzel should be stopped from peddling deception and error. Note Luther's direct attack on the "preachers of indulgences" in thesis 21:

> Therefore those preachers of indulgences are in error, who say that by the pope's indulgences a man is freed from every penalty, and saved.

In thesis 28 he attacks the crass sloganeering of the preachers of indulgences:

It is certain that when the penny jingles into the money-box, gain and avarice can be increased, but the result of the intercession of the Church is in the power of God alone.

With his Ninety-Five Theses, Luther, whether he intended it or not at the time, had launched the first salvo of what would become the Protestant Reformation.

The Aftermath of the Ninety-Five Theses

Historical evidence suggests that Luther was not intent on creating a revolution by means of his Ninety-Five Theses. It is much more likely that Luther simply desired an academic disputation on these issues. But, in modern parlance, Luther's Ninety-Five Theses went viral in Germany, and within two weeks after affixing them to the door of the Castle Church at Wittenberg, they had circulated throughout the entire country!

Luther took no rash actions in response to his newfound fame. He continued to preach and teach the Scriptures. During 1517, he lectured on Galatians and further refined his theology. After Galatians, Luther ventured into Hebrews. He did what he always did—he applied himself to the labor at hand with great diligence.

Although Luther tended to his teaching with great diligence, this is not to say that he ceased from addressing the topic of indulgences. To the contrary, Luther addressed the subject directly in his preaching. The most famous example of this came in his message titled "Sermon on Indulgences and Grace," which was published in early 1518. This sermon would later become a best-seller during the height of the Reformation. In this sermon, Luther continued to call into question the efficacy of indulgences with regard to providing the believer with forgiveness. He spoke of the theology of indulgences as a "grievous error." Luther directed his hearers to God's Word and what it stated about forgiveness. He noted the importance of God's unmerited favor in granting forgiveness and turned his listeners away from attempting to earn forgiveness through indulgences or spectacular acts of contrition. In this sermon, Luther set in the ground two pillars of the Reformation to come—the emphasis on God's grace in salvation and the authority of God's Word over the teachings of men. It was these ideas, rather than the

Ninety-Five Theses per se, that made Luther such a dangerous man in the eyes of the pope and the religious establishment of his day.

Unsurprisingly, Luther's "Sermon on Indulgences and Grace" came to the attention of the pope. The sermon was immediately viewed as error that the church had to counter with full force. In 1518, the Dominican Sylvester Mazzolini, also known as Prierias (a name he earned from his birthplace of Prierio), was charged with the task of responding to the errors of the German monk. Prierias was a highly regarded theologian and would later serve as the judge in Luther's trial for heresy. He was a capable and formidable foe, and he took up his task with great zeal.

Prierias's response to Luther came in the form of his *Dialogue Concerning the Power of the Pope*. It is noteworthy that the germane issue that sent ripples through the Vatican hierarchy was not indulgences but the broader concerns of papal authority. Prierias recognized that if Luther's position was not condemned, then the entire authority structure of the church would be in question. Accordingly, Prierias focused his response on the deeper issue of the pope's authority to dictate the doctrine and practices of the church, including his power to grant indulgences.

Prierias's response set forth unequivocally the position that the pope, when making decisions in his office as pope, could not err. Once the pope set his seal on a decision pertaining to the life and doctrine of the church, it was, per se, correct and infallible. This position, of course, meant that any questioning of a papal decision was immediately considered as error and potentially as heresy. Luther was on his way to being branded a heretic. Prierias's *Dialogue* ensured that conflict could not be avoided and that there was no room for a compromise. Luther would not get his desired dialogue on this issue. He had only two options—recant or risk being convicted of heresy.

Luther responded to Prierias's *Dialogue* by attacking all of its presuppositions and arguments. He employed canon law and the church fathers, including the venerable Augustine, to refute Prierias's position on papal infallibility. Instead, Luther argued that the teaching of the church, its law, its fathers, and of Scripture itself is that the only infallible rule for faith and life is the Bible. Luther posited that there is an authority higher than the pope—namely, the Holy Scriptures. Luther's response further entrenched the two parties and placed them even more at odds. The stage was being set for a showdown between Luther and the most powerful institution in all of Europe.

Luther Is Summoned to Rome

When Luther received his copy of Prierias's *Dialogue*, it was accompanied by a summons requiring him to appear in Rome for examination within sixty days. This represented a significant escalation in Rome's response to Luther, and it was clear to him that his life was at risk. The summons noted that he was to answer to charges of heresy. This was serious, and Luther knew it. He rightly feared going to Rome.

Luther's immediate response to the summons was to attempt to change the venue of the hearing from hostile Rome to his friendly Germany. He appealed to his friend Georg Spalatin, then the secretary to Frederick the Wise, to expedite his request for the trial to be held in Germany. Luther knew if he went to Rome he might not return. His hope for an academic disputation on the topic of indulgences and church authority was dashed.

This was becoming a legal matter of the highest consequence, and even his life was at stake.

While Luther was pulling the levers of local political power, he received a papal letter indicating that he would not be required to travel to Rome if he was willing to publicly recant his errors before Cardinal Thomas Cajetan in Augsburg, Germany. If Luther failed to recant, then the cardinal was authorized to send him to Rome in chains. A disputation would not be afforded Luther. Instead, he had a very simple choice: recant or be carried off to Rome against his will. Luther was faced with his first life-or-death decision regarding his beliefs and his commitment to them.

Frederick the Wise was aware of the peril that Luther was facing, and he came to the aid of his resident theologian. When Luther left for Augsburg, he did not leave alone. He was afforded quality legal counsel. Even though he was relieved to have the hearing in Germany, he still feared for his life. In fact, Luther's comments regarding this period of his life indicate that he believed this would be a one-way trip from which he would never return. Luther believed he was walking to his death.

When Luther appeared before Cajetan in Augsburg, he faced a resilient and indefatigable opponent. He was consistently peppered with demands to recant but refused to do so in the absence of scriptural evidence. The two men were at an impasse. But Luther was not turned over to Rome; instead, he received what he referred to as his "first excommunication." His good friend and mentor, Johann von Staupitz, removed Luther from the Augustinian order. This removal put a stay on the summons to Rome and the charges against him.

On October 20, 1518, almost one year from his posting of the Ninety-Five Theses, Luther made a hasty exit from Augsburg. He galloped on his unsaddled horse furiously throughout the night until he was utterly exhausted. When he dismounted from the horse, Luther could barely walk. He realized that he had, at least temporarily, received a stay of execution. His battle with Rome, however, was far from over.

Luther Loses His Protector?

On October 31, 1518, on the one-year anniversary of his Ninety-Five Theses, Luther arrived in Wittenberg, his safe haven and home. Unbeknownst to Luther, after he fled Augsburg and his battle with Cajetan, the cardinal wrote a forceful letter to Luther's protector, Frederick the Wise of Saxony. In the letter, Cajetan recounted the exchange with Luther, skewing the facts in his favor, and pressured Frederick to stop protecting Luther. Cajetan referred to Luther as a "monk of no account," emphasizing that he was not a worthy recipient of Frederick's costly political capital. Cajetan, in not subtle ways, attempted to put Frederick in fear. For example, at the end of the letter, Cajetan noted how sad it would be if Frederick were to suffer a blemish on his glorious record due to this monk of no account. He could save face by either ejecting Luther from his territories or by sending him to Rome to face the charges against him. Frederick was now under great pressure. Through Cardinal Cajetan, Rome was increasingly intimidating the elector of Saxony.

But Frederick was not the only person with whom Cajetan corresponded in the wake of the Augsburg confrontation. Cajetan sent a second letter to Rome noting Luther's refusal to recant. This report resulted in renewed assaults against him. First, Prierias penned another attack on Luther and his teachings. Even more troubling for Luther, however, was what occurred on December 13, 1518. On that day, *Cum Postquam*, a new papal decree, was issued stating unequivocally that the pope's authority extended to the area of indulgences. In other words, the papal decree affirmed that the pope had authority to issue indulgences at will and that to deny this would make one a heretic. It specifically denounced any preachers who would dare teach against the substance of this decree. Although Luther was not mentioned by name, it was clear that the German monk was the target. He may have won his battle with Cajetan in Augsburg, but with the issuing of *Cum Postquam* it seemed obvious to all that Cajetan was about to win the war. The decree provided Luther with little recourse. The matter of indulgences was not open for debate. To question the pope's authority to issue indulgences was to question the pope's authority—period.

Luther was not the only person facing coercion from Rome. Frederick continued to feel the pressure to remove his protection of Luther. He sent Luther a copy of the letter he received from Cajetan and requested Luther's response. Luther provided a spirited reply to Cajetan's letter and vigorously defended himself to Frederick. He noted that his desire was simply to defend and debate the truth but that Cajetan denied him the opportunity to do so. Although Luther defended himself to Frederick, he began to fear that Frederick was about to give in to the pressure from Rome. He steeled himself for a possible evacuation from Wittenberg and from Saxony. He contemplated fleeing to France and began corresponding with his close friends. He was preparing for the end of Frederick's favor. In his letter to Frederick, Luther even went as far as to offer to voluntarily leave his territories if requested to do so.

Luther awaited Frederick's response with trepidation, expecting that he would be required to flee. But on December 18, 1518, he received a letter from Frederick noting that Luther's letter to him had convinced him that he was doing the right thing in protecting Luther. Frederick pledged to continue to shield his pesky little monk. Luther would not be heading to Rome.

Chapter 5
The Heat of Battle

In the wake of the Augsburg confrontation, the immediate sense of the threat against Luther waned with the assurance that Frederick was still his protector, and he again returned to his studies. During 1519, the University of Wittenberg became a center for theological debate, particularly for those critical of certain aspects of the Church of Rome. In a sense, Wittenberg was becoming a Lutheran university, taking on his character and passion. Needless to say, Luther himself was clearly the most influential member of the faculty.

The Wisdom of Wittenberg and the Fury of Eck
Although Luther was the visible leader of Wittenberg, he was by no means alone. Two of Luther's most prominent colleagues were Andreas Karlstadt (1486–1541) and Philip Melanchthon (1497–1560). Karlstadt surpassed Luther in both age and bravado.

Although an accomplished scholar, Karlstadt often allowed his passions to undermine his erudition. He was so controversial at times in his views, criticisms, and methods that even Luther deemed him excessive. Melanchthon, on the other hand, was an entirely different person. He was small in stature but a giant in terms of his scholarship and intelligence. Luther admired him. Melanchthon, in turn, was devoted to Luther and credited Luther's interpretation of the apostle Paul as being instrumental in his own conversion. The three men championed Luther's teachings, and the reputation of Wittenberg prospered, but it was not unopposed.

Luther and his colleagues at Wittenberg were challenged by Johann Eck of the University of Ingolstadt. Eck was not a new foe for Luther. After Luther posted his Ninety-Five Theses, Eck attacked the German monk and his teachings in print through his *Obelisks*. Luther was quite offended by Eck's opposition and countered him in writing. He was surprised that a German would attack him in this manner. He expected this type of attack from the Italians in Rome but not from his fellow countrymen. What perturbed him even more was that Luther, prior to this exchange, had counted Eck a friend. There was for Luther a sense of personal betrayal in Eck's opposition.

Johann Eck was a capable opponent for the doctors of Wittenberg. He not only was a capable scholar and debater but was also very good at organizing opposition to Wittenberg. Eck quite cleverly recruited the University of Leipzig to join in the fight on his side. Leipzig was a rival school to Wittenberg and perhaps was jealous of its newfound success. There Eck found a welcome response to his overtures to oppose Wittenberg.

Eck began a campaign to entice Luther to debate him. At first, the brash Karlstadt stepped forward expressing a desire to spar with Eck. After all, Karlstadt had already issued a ferocious attack against Eck and was all too eager to enter the ring with him. Eck, however, was not willing to settle on debating with one of Luther's lieutenants; instead, Eck demanded that Luther step forward and debate him. Finally, Luther could no longer fend off Eck's persistent demands for a public debate. He consented to debate Eck at the University of Leipzig for what became known as the Leipzig Debate.

The Leipzig Debate

The Leipzig Debate was held during the heat of July 1519. With confidence, Eck arrived ahead of Luther and his entourage from Wittenberg. Luther's most trusted allies, Karlstadt and Melanchthon, were both by his side. Reportedly, Luther also was accompanied by hundreds of fully armed students to provide for his defense. In turn, Eck received aid from Leipzig in the form of seventy-six armed guards. It was quite a scene. The tension was high.

Leipzig was not that far from Prague, the place where Jan Hus had been martyred in 1415 in response to his calls for reforming the papacy. Eck was interested in painting Luther as Hus's successor, and it was not a characterization that Luther resisted. Luther was quite willing to be seen as following in the footsteps of Hus, and he embraced all efforts by Eck to portray him in this manner.

The debate began with the two sides fighting over the terms and structure of the debate. They trifled over issues such as whether stenographers should be used and how the debate should be judged. Eventually, they decided on the universities of Paris and Erfurt as the appropriate judges.

The debate in Leipzig began with Eck squaring off against Karlstadt. The debate was broad in its theological scope and addressed a variety of topics that were not directly related to the authority of the papacy or the selling of indulgences. For example, the debate began with an extended exchange over the respective roles and contributions of free will and grace in the performance of good works on the part of believers. But then the main event commenced as Eck and Luther went toe-to-toe over the authority of the papacy. Luther advocated a position that acknowledged papal authority but limited it to being of human grant and origins rather than from divine fiat. In other words, Luther contended that the pope's authority was one granted to him by the church and not from God. Eck was quick to seize on Luther's position and argue that the German monk was undermining the doctrine of the church through his subversive teachings. The two men continued to spar over the issue of papal authority. Eck even produced letters purporting to establish the connection of the papacy to the apostle Peter, but Luther was not persuaded. This is when Eck pressed the comparisons between Luther and Hus. The tension was palpable.

The debate continued with great fervor. Other topics were addressed, such as the biblical basis for purgatory and the granting of indulgences, but the debates continually circled back to the issue of authority: Is it the pope or the Bible that has the final say on matters of theology? Luther, of course, argued that popes and councils could and do err and that the Bible is the only true authority to guide faith and life. Eck attacked Luther for denying the divine authority granted to the papacy and painted his views as radical.

After eighteen days, the debate finally came to a close, although many witnesses recounted that it could have proceeded indefinitely. The two men were indefatigable. Even though the oral debate had ceased, the two sides continued to launch salvos at one another by means of pamphlets.

The debate ended with both sides becoming further entrenched in their original positions. Eck reported to Rome that Luther was the "Saxon Hus" and should be treated in like manner by the church. Luther, in turn, came to embrace more and more the title that Eck was so interested in bestowing on him. During his time in Leipzig, Luther became more acquainted and conversant in the writings and positions of Jan Hus, leaving Leipzig with a profound sense that he was indeed a successor to the man and his thought. He was very pleased to be called the Saxon Hus and wore the title with pride.

Exsurge Domine

Pope Leo X determined that it was time to strike back at this rebellious monk from Saxony. He assembled a team of scholars to respond to Luther's teachings, which culminated in the publishing of a papal bull on June 15, 1520—*Exsurge Domine.*

Exsurge Domine was written as a purposely forceful and forthright rebuke against the "errors" coming from Germany. While it cast a wide net to include all the "heretics" of Wittenberg, it left no doubt that the prime target was Luther. The first part of the attack was against his writings:

> Moreover, because the preceding errors and many others are contained in the books or writings of Martin Luther, we likewise condemn, reprobate, and reject completely the books and all the writings and sermons of the said Martin, whether in Latin or any other language, containing the said errors or any one of them; and we wish them to be

regarded as utterly condemned, reprobated, and rejected. We forbid each and every one of the faithful of either sex, in virtue of holy obedience and under the above penalties to be incurred automatically, to read, assert, preach, praise, print, publish, or defend them. They will incur these penalties if they presume to uphold them in any way, personally or through another or others, directly or indirectly, tacitly or explicitly, publicly or occultly, either in their own homes or in other public or private places. Indeed immediately after the publication of this letter these works, wherever they may be, shall be sought out carefully by the ordinaries and others [ecclesiastics and regulars], and under each and every one of the above penalties shall be burned publicly and solemnly in the presence of the clerics and people.

The next part of the attack against Luther was personal:

As far as Martin himself is concerned, O good God, what have we overlooked or not done? What fatherly charity have we omitted that we might call him back from such errors? For after we had cited him, wishing to deal more kindly with him, we urged him through various conferences with our legate and through our personal letters to abandon these errors. We have even offered him safe conduct and the money necessary for the journey urging him to come without fear or any misgivings, which perfect charity should cast out, and to talk not secretly but openly and face to face after the example of our Savior and the Apostle Paul. If he had done this, we are certain he would have changed in heart, and he would have recognized his errors. He would not have found all these errors in the Roman Curia which he attacks so viciously, ascribing to it more than he should because of the empty rumors of wicked men. We would have shown him clearer than the light of day that the Roman pontiffs, our predecessors, whom he injuriously attacks beyond all decency, never erred in their canons or constitutions which he tries to assail. For, according to the prophet, neither is healing oil nor the doctor lacking in Galaad. But he always refused to listen and, despising the previous citation and each and every one of the above overtures, disdained to come. To the present day he has been contumacious. With a hardened spirit he has continued under censure over a year. What is worse, adding evil to evil, and on learning of the citation, he broke forth in a rash appeal to a future council. This to be sure was contrary to the constitution of Pius II and Julius II our predecessors that all appealing in this way are to be punished with the penalties of heretics. In vain does he implore the help of a council, since he openly admits that he does not believe in a council.

Finally, Luther received his ultimatum:

Therefore we can, without any further citation or delay, proceed against him to his condemnation and damnation as one whose faith is notoriously suspect and in fact a true heretic with the full severity of each and all of the above penalties and censures. Yet, with the advice of our brothers, imitating the mercy of almighty God who does not wish the death of a sinner but rather that he be converted and live, and forgetting all the injuries inflicted on us and the Apostolic See, we have decided to use all the compassion we are capable of. It is our hope, so far as in us lies, that he will experience a change of heart by taking the road of mildness we have proposed, return, and turn away from his errors. We will receive him kindly as the prodigal son returning to the embrace of the Church.

Therefore let Martin himself and all those adhering to him, and those who shelter and support him, through the merciful heart of our God and the sprinkling of the blood of our Lord Jesus Christ by which and through whom the redemption of the human race and the upbuilding of holy mother Church was accomplished, know that from our heart we exhort and beseech that he cease to disturb the peace, unity, and truth of the Church for which the Savior prayed so earnestly to the Father. Let him abstain from his pernicious errors that he may come back to us. If they really will obey, and certify to us by legal documents that they have obeyed, they will find in us the affection of a father's love, the opening of the font of the effects of paternal charity, and opening of the font of mercy and clemency.

We enjoin, however, on Martin that in the meantime he cease from all preaching or the office of preacher.[1]

With the publication of *Exsurge Domine* Luther's choice was clear, and the focus shifted to how he would respond. Would he recant and return as a prodigal son to the pope, or suffer the fate of one declared a heretic?

Luther's Response to *Exsurge Domine*

With the issuing of *Exsurge Domine* the conflict between Luther and the papacy was reaching increased levels of tension. That tension was about to increase as Luther contemplated and issued his response. Instead of recanting, Luther furthered his rebellion through his own written responses.

Although *Exsurge Domine* was issued in June 1520, it did not reach Luther until December of that same year. Between June and October of 1520 rumors began to spread about the papal bull and the threat of Luther's excommunication. He used

---

1. The entire encyclical may be found at http://www .papalencyclicals.net/Leo10/l10exdom.htm.

the intervening months to pen a series of tracts criticizing the papacy and the Church of Rome.

The first of these tracts was *Address to the German Nobility*. In this tract, Luther called on the civil magistrates of Germany to assist in the reformation of the Church of Rome. Luther spoke of three walls of Rome that must be crumbled like the walls of Jericho: The first wall was the idea that the Church of Rome was not under the jurisdiction of temporal powers, such as the German magistrates. The second wall was the position that only the pope could interpret the meaning of the Scriptures. The third was the principle that only the pope could call a council to debate matters of faith. Luther called on the German nobility to resist these claims as false. He trumpeted the power of the state and the priesthood of all believers. By means of this tract, Luther summoned the leaders of his homeland to resist the power of the papacy.

The second major tract was *On the Babylonian Captivity of the Church*. It focused on theological matters, particularly the power and efficacy of the sacraments. Luther launched an attack on the idea that the Eucharist represented an actual sacrificial act, noting that the Bible taught that the Lord's

Supper is a sacrament, not a sacrifice. He also contended that Christ instituted only two sacraments, whereas Rome claimed there were seven. This tract was Luther's clarion call for the reformation of the sacraments and the sacramental system. It was written in a style and tone that left no doubt it was a frontal assault on the pope and the Church of Rome.

The third major tract was *The Freedom of a Christian*. In this profound tract, Luther set forth the basic Protestant idea of Christian liberty; that is, that the Christian has been set free by Christ from sin, Satan, and death. This freedom, rather than producing license, instead produces liberty to live for Christ by submitting to other believers and legitimate authorities. This tract had a conciliatory tone compared with the *Babylonian Captivity*, but it proved just as powerful an attack against the status quo of the Church of Rome.

After publishing this series of tracts, Luther finally received his official copy of *Exsurge Domine* on December 10, 1520. As part of the campaign against Luther, the pope had commanded the burning of his books and sermons. Luther chose to follow suit and summarily took the papal bull and burned it in the presence of his friends and students at Elster Gate in Wittenberg.

Excommunication

Hostilities between Luther and the pope had reached a climax. The pope had issued his *Exsurge Domine*, and Luther had parried with his three tracts. Both sides had burned the writings of the other. Both sides were marshaling their forces. Then, on January 3, 1521, Pope Leo X chose to formally employ what he had earlier threatened in *Exsurge Domine*. By means of a papal bull, *Decet Romanum Pontificem*, Luther was officially excommunicated from the church. For Luther, there was now no turning back.

Chapter 6
The Diet of Worms

Pope Leo's excommunication of Luther put the Reformer in a serious predicament. The pressure on Luther, and on those protecting him, was increasing. Frederick the Wise, the elector of Saxony, continued to be resolute in his defense of Luther and advocated that he at least deserved a fair hearing on the issues. Frederick, however, was not the only political leader who had jurisdiction over Luther. Charles V, the Holy Roman emperor, was also a player when it came to the politics of Martin Luther.

Charles V was held in disfavor by the pope even before Luther began causing trouble with his reforms and controversial writings. The pope feared that too much power was being concentrated in the office of the Holy Roman emperor and that Charles V was becoming a rival to the papacy. In turn, Charles V had displayed his hostility toward Rome when he had his armies march on the Vatican and briefly took the pope as his prisoner.

While the story of Martin Luther revolves around theological matters, one cannot understand the unfolding story of his life without also recognizing the politically charged environment in which Luther found himself. In our world, particularly in modern Western democracies, we often view religious and political matters as occupying separate spheres. It was not so in the time of Luther. Luther's attacks against Rome and the papacy had clear political implications. If Luther prevailed, papal power over Europe would be struck a serious blow. Frederick knew this, Charles V knew this, and Pope Leo X also knew it. The stakes were high, and Luther was in the center of it all.

A Hearing for the German Monk

Charles V was struggling to hold together the loose confederation of his empire. He had to balance a variety of interests internally within Europe, particularly the rivalry Germany had with France, and was also well aware of the increasing threat posed by the Ottoman Turks. In 1520, the Turks had made significant incursions into Europe, conquering the cities of Buda and Pest and laying siege to Vienna. Luther's conflict with Rome was just one of the many crises that Charles V was juggling, but it got his attention. Charles V entered into a dialogue with Frederick of Saxony over the fate of Luther. The issue was whether Luther should be turned over to Rome or offered a hearing on the issues and charges against him. It was not lost on Charles V that just two years earlier Frederick had put him into his office by casting the deciding vote in his favor. Frederick prevailed, and Charles V agreed to grant the German monk a hearing.

One of the powers of the Holy Roman emperor was the ability to assemble political leaders within his jurisdiction for the purpose of resolving great issues. These assemblies were referred to as "diets." In April 1521, Charles V exercised this power and called the Diet of Worms, so named because the assembly was to be held in the German city of Worms. Charles V issued a summons to the German monk to appear before the Diet of Worms and ensured Luther he would be guaranteed safe passage.

When Luther received the summons, he was clearly uncertain of the purpose or intentions of Charles V and his diet. Was the purpose to force him to recant? Luther was resolute against doing that. Would he be arrested and turned over to the pope or summarily executed upon arrival? He actually preferred this option to being pressured to recant his views. Would he, perhaps, actually be allowed an opportunity to present his case and justify his position? Luther decided to submit to the summons and made his way to the city of Worms, unsure of whether he would be making a return trip.

The Diet of Worms

On April 16, 1521, Martin Luther arrived at Worms. Although accompanied by only a small group, he was welcomed by nearly two thousand people. While Luther was a nuisance to the pope and a cause of political anxiety for the leaders of Europe, he was revered and beloved by the people of Germany.

The next day, around four o'clock in the afternoon, Luther was secretly taken to the meeting place in order to avoid inciting the crowds. He was brought into the presence of some of the most powerful leaders of his age. It was an intimidating setting to say the least.

The emperor's representative made two direct and curt inquiries of Luther. The emperor first asked Luther if he had authored the books that they had sequestered prior to him arriving at the diet. He readily confirmed that he was indeed the author of the books in question.

The second question directed at Luther was whether he still stood by his writings, or if he now desired to recant his views. That was the key question: Would Luther recant? Many at the Diet of Worms hoped that he would. For them, a recantation by Luther would solve their problems and reduce the tensions with Rome. If Luther recanted, they could all go home and deal with what they saw as more pressing concerns. A great silence fell on the room. Luther did not immediately respond. Although often given to quick and crass retorts, Luther restrained himself in this esteemed setting. When he finally spoke, it was not to give an answer but to request more time to give his answer. His request was granted. Luther had twenty-four hours to consider his reply—to consider whether he wished to live or die.

The next day, April 18, 1521, Luther was again brought before the tribunal. His twenty-four hours were up, and it was time to give his answer. Silence once again filled the hall as everyone awaited the monk's response. Luther was sweating and suffering under the tremendous stress of the situation. Then Luther sounded forth in the German tongue with what has become his most memorable recorded statement:

> Unless I am convinced by the testimony of the Holy Scriptures or by evident reason—for I can believe neither pope nor councils alone, as it is clear that they have erred repeatedly and contradicted themselves—I consider myself convicted by the testimony of Holy Scripture, which is my basis; my conscience is captive to the Word of God. Thus I cannot and will not recant, because acting against one's conscience is neither safe nor sound. God help me. Amen.[1]

---

1. Heiko A. Oberman, *Luther: Man between God and the Devil* (New Haven, Conn.: Yale University Press, 2006), 39.

Luther did not recant. He stood by his views and principles. Before the most powerful people of his time, Luther stood firm and true even though he knew that such a stance would likely result in his execution. He understood the gravity of his decision. He nearly broke down from exhaustion when asked to repeat his statement in Latin for the record. He was shepherded summarily from the room, and hisses of condemnation followed him out of the presence of the angered electors of the Diet of Worms.

The Edict of Worms

After Luther's departure, Charles V called on his electors to offer their opinions on what should be done with him. In essence, he called on them for a verdict. The electors fell silent and begged for more time to consider their thoughts before rendering them. The young emperor curtly interrupted them and declared that he was ready to render his opinion on the matter. Charles V then unleashed a forceful and unequivocal condemnation of Luther and his views. He forcefully declared his intention to treat Luther as a heretic, and he summoned the six electors to join with him. While Charles's condemnation of Luther may at first seem odd given his past disagreements with Rome, it is important to remember that he was a devout Catholic and would also benefit politically by ridding himself of the problem of Martin Luther. If Charles condemned Luther to death, Rome would be indebted to him and he would have brought an end to Luther stirring up his own German subjects with his writings. Four of the six electors concurred with Charles's verdict. Frederick the Wise, however, was among those who showed his dissent by refusing to sign off on the emperor's decision.

Charles V believed he had sufficient support to execute his judgment on Luther. In the meantime, however, tensions among the peasants of Germany were growing. Luther had become a representative of the common man. He was one man standing up against power and wealth. He was incredibly popular among the masses, and any condemnation of Luther could incite a peasant uprising. The local German officials recognized this threat and pleaded with Charles V to give Luther a second hearing. The emperor brushed off these pleas and noted that he had no intention of hearing the heretic again. But he also recognized the political realities of the situation, particularly the risks inherent in making Luther a martyr. Given these political realities, Charles acquiesced to the pleas of the local German officials and allowed for a second hearing in their presence. The officials hoped they could broker a peace between Luther and Rome and simultaneously avert a peasant revolt.

The committee members that met with Luther were tireless in their attempts to persuade the monk to recant. Luther would not budge. His resolve was just as firm as it was in the presence of the emperor. After three days, the committee reported to the emperor and noted its inability to persuade Luther to recant.

Charles V next proceeded to formalize his verdict and sentence against Luther. The product of this was the Edict of Worms. Issued on May 8, 1521, it was forceful and comprehensive in its denunciation of Luther and his teaching. The edict notes the fairness of the tribunal in providing Luther safe travel and due process. It references the opportunity offered to Luther to recant and also notes his repeated refusal to do so. It lists a bill of particulars regarding the various aberrant teachings of Luther, noting particularly his attacks on the sacraments and the sacramental system of the Church of Rome. The edict also notes Luther's disparagement of the pope himself. After noting the list of his offenses the edict declares,

> To put an end to the numberless and end-less errors of the said Martin, let us say that it seems that this man, Martin, is not a man but a demon in the appearance of a man, clothed in religious habit to be better able to deceive mankind, and wanting to gather the heresies of several heretics who have already been condemned, excommunicated, and bur-ied in hell for a long time. Let us add to this all the heresies recently brought in by him to be the source of all iniquity and rubbish and to destroy the Catholic faith. As an evangeli-cal preacher he labors to trouble and demolish all religious peace and charity and all order and direction in the things of this world. And finally, he brings dishonor upon all the beauty of our Holy Mother Church.

The edict then confirms that Luther is a heretic worthy of excommunication:

First of all, to the honor of Almighty God, in reverence both to his vicar here on earth, our Holy Father the pope, and to the Holy Apostolic See, moved by zeal, affection, and our natural inclination, and in imitation of our predecessors, we appeal to the defense of the Catholic faith and to the protection of the Holy Roman Church. We desire to defend our goods, to use our power, our domains, our friends and subjects, and if necessary, to risk our own life and blood and whatever it pleases God to give us in this world. By the authority vested in us, and upon the advice of the princes, prelates, knights of our orders, and gentlemen of our council gathered here in great numbers, we have ordered that mandates be sent to every one of our chancelleries and domains in their own language by which the sentence is to be executed against Martin Luther and his false doctrine (already condemned by our Holy Father the pope, the true and legitimate judge in these matters), as contained in the above-mentioned bulls presented to us. We have declared and hereby forever declare by this edict that the said Martin Luther is to be considered an estranged

member, rotten and cut off from the body of
our Holy Mother Church. He is an obstinate,
schismatic, and we want him to be
considered as such by all of you.[2]

With the publication of the Edict of Worms,
the charges of Pope Leo X had been confirmed
by the political leaders of Europe. It seemed that
the pope had won a great victory and that Luther's
demise was imminent—but neither turned out to
be the case.

From Worms to Wartburg

Oddly enough, not much happened after the Edict
of Worms was issued. Charles V returned to what
he considered were more important matters and
was not consumed with following up on the pesky
German monk. Of course, Charles had other reasons to avoid taking any further action against
Luther given the risk of this causing a peasant
revolt in Germany. Many historians believe that
the purpose of the Edict of Worms was simply to

---

2. The text of the Edict of Worms is from a translation prepared by Dennis Bratcher, which appears at http://www.crivoice
.org/creededictworms.html.

silence Luther and his criticisms. Essentially, it was meant to be an idle threat. The hope was that it would have a chilling effect among Luther and his supporters and that they would simply disappear.

Luther did in fact disappear for a time at the behest of Frederick the Wise. Frederick once again extended protection to his favorite monk. While the Edict of Worms may have been meaningless for the politicians of Europe, for Rome it served as vindication of its sentence. Luther stood condemned as a heretic by the church and by the state. His life was at risk.

Frederick's plan was to essentially kidnap the monk and hide him in a safe place. In a scene befit for a Hollywood movie, Luther was whisked away under darkness, ascending a winding road to Wartburg Castle, which would become his new home. It seemed for a moment that the pope and the emperor had succeeded in neutralizing Luther. That moment would soon pass.

Chapter 7

From Wartburg to Wittenberg

The castle at Wartburg was a formidable structure. It was a fortress that served to protect Luther from his enemies, but it was also a place of imprisonment. Luther's friends were unaware of his location, and when they received letters from him they were addressed from places such as "the wilderness" or the "Isle of Patmos." Luther was hidden and isolated.

Luther Struggles at Wartburg

Luther did not welcome his isolation at Wartburg. He was thankful to be alive and to be afforded the gracious protection once again offered by Frederick the Wise, but he was also filled with depression and anxiety over what he saw as an incarceration. He did not want to be at Wartburg but rather desired to return to Wittenberg to continue his work and to be among his comrades. He missed the fellowship of his friends.

Wartburg was not a happy place. Luther was assigned to a room in a dark, dank castle that was in a state of disrepair. Bats, owls, and other critters made their home in the castle, and they often startled Luther, adding to his feeling of foreboding. He often remarked about how he felt the devil's presence and how the devil tormented him while at Wartburg. At one point, Luther reportedly threw an inkwell at the devil, which crashed against the wall, leaving a mark. The darkness of Wartburg began to leave a mark on Luther, and he entered into a period of personal and inward darkness.

Luther felt torment not only from the devil but also from himself. He began to have doubts and likened himself to Noah: just as Noah seemed crazy in his time, Luther began to feel the same way. He began to question whether he was really hearing and following God or if he had been misguided in his convictions and teachings. With loneliness, isolation, depression, and anxiety tormenting the sum of his experience at Wartburg, he entered into a period of spiraling self-doubt.

In addition to these spiritual and psychological challenges, Luther was struggling physically. He suffered from stomach ailments, constipation, and insomnia. He felt lousy, and his restricted circumstances curtailed his exposure to fresh air, fresh food, and exercise. In short, he was miserable.

Luther Works at Wartburg

Despite his many struggles at Wartburg, Luther was actually quite productive during his time there. His tenacious nature emerged again as he committed himself tirelessly to his work.

One of the massive projects Luther undertook during this period was translating the New Testament from its original Greek into German. This was a daunting and radical task. Translation work was not one of Luther's great strengths. He recognized that his friend Melanchthon was much more gifted in this discipline, but Luther pressed on with the task. Amazingly, he completed his work in about eleven weeks' time! Luther's German New Testament would become a standard text in Germany for centuries after his time at Wartburg.

The War Continues at Wittenberg

Even though Luther was isolated at Wartburg, he was not neutralized. The Reformation continued to gain momentum, and the heart of activity was still centered in Wittenberg. He was kept fully abreast of the goings-on at Wittenberg, and his counsel was solicited regarding major issues as they arose.

One of the major rebellions against Rome that arose while Luther was at Wartburg was that the clergy began to marry. Luther had advocated for this position, noting that the Bible included no prohibition against clergy being married. Luther believed the opposite was true, that the clergy should be married. While he was at Wartburg, this began to be realized, particularly around Wittenberg. Monks even began to marry nuns! The world was changing.

Another powerful change that occurred during this time is that the priests began to share the cup with the laity during the celebration of the Eucharist. Luther had also advocated this change, noting that the cup was for the people and that the celebration of the Lord's Supper was not a sacrifice.

Other reforms included changing the liturgical language of the church service from Latin to German, ceasing to require clergy to wear priestly vestments, eating meat during church-designated days of fasting, and terminating the practice of saying Masses for the dead. The floodgates of change seemed to be springing open while Luther remained locked behind the gate of Wartburg Castle.

Luther welcomed these reforms, but not without some caution. He worried that the people were becoming preoccupied with these outward statements of rebellion and religious liberty and were forgetting the core doctrines that gave rise to them. Luther always faced the struggle that his reforms could be welcomed for either religious reasons or political reasons. The leaders of Germany were tired of giving homage to the pope, and the peasants resented the wealth and pageantry of Rome. Joining in a rebellion against the papacy was a very popular idea in Germany, and Luther feared that people were losing sight of the core principles of the Reformation.

Although Luther had some reservations regarding the reforms, he did not voice these publicly and did not cease from spurring on such reforms. While at Wartburg he wrote several tracts on suggested reforms, including the elimination of monastic vows and the abolishment of the celebration of private Masses. But Luther began to notice that his tracts were not being put into broader circulation and had also learned that some in Wittenberg were taking his reforms far beyond his original intent. He decided to come out of hiding and to make a trip to Wittenberg to investigate these issues.

Wittenberg Becomes Radicalized

In December of 1521, Luther made a clandestine journey back to Wittenberg. During his time at the castle, his hair had grown quite long and he also grew a beard. These changed his physical appearance significantly and helped him to sneak into Wittenberg undetected. The city was abuzz with talk about Luther and speculation regarding his location. Wittenberg was also bustling with radical activity. Luther's reforms were taking hold, and some people were intent on taking his reforms to extremes that he neither intended nor desired.

Things continued to heat up in Wittenberg after Luther's secret and short visit. Extreme factions began to form. One of the leading extremists was a friend and colleague of Luther. Andreas Karlstadt was a faculty member at the University at Wittenberg who had stood with Luther on many occasions. Karlstadt, who had initially resisted the reforms of Luther, later embraced them with great passion. He eventually came to the conclusion that Luther actually had not gone far enough in his reforms, and he resolved to correct this error. He took up the mantle of the leader of what became known as the Radical Reformation.

One extreme position advocated by Karlstadt was related to the power of the Holy Spirit and the interpretation of Scripture. Luther had advocated for the idea that the Scriptures were plain and could be understood by the laity. Karlstadt took this core idea and built on it by contending that the Holy Spirit spoke to each individual and that the laity could interpret the Scriptures exclusive of help from trained clergy.

In addition to Karlstadt's radicalism, Luther's former students were also causing trouble in Wittenberg. The day prior to Luther's arrival they had engaged in a riot that involved the use of weapons. They invaded a local parish church and drove the priests out. On Christmas Eve of 1521, Karlstadt's supporters engaged in a similar riot.

Tensions were high in Wittenberg. On Christmas Day, nearly two thousand people assembled for a Mass led by Karlstadt at Castle Church. Karlstadt wore no priestly vestments, radically altered the eucharistic liturgy to make it devoid of reference to sacrifice, and performed part of the service in the German tongue. At one level this was an amazing moment; for the first time in many of the participants' lives they actually understood what the priest was saying during the Mass. Karlstadt then distributed both the bread and the cup to the people. Again, this was momentous as the laity had never had this level of access to both elements of the sacrament.

Karlstadt's radical actions on that Christmas soon became codified practices in Wittenberg. The political leaders of the town, who were under severe pressure from Karlstadt and his swelling ranks of supporters, essentially embraced all of what Karlstadt mandated. They also included a provision to remove all vain images from the churches. Music, particularly the use of the organ, also came under attack. Karlstadt and his supporters took up the task of ridding the church of images and instruments.

But Karlstadt was bested by other, even more radicalized Reformers. Leaders arose who claimed prophetic gifts and divine knowledge. They claimed that God spoke to them directly and so they had no need of the Bible at all. They argued against the practice of infant baptism and called for its abolishment. Many of these so-called prophets predicted that the end of the age was near and that Jesus's return was imminent.

Groups known as Anabaptists began advocating the rebaptism of adults who were baptized as children. They contended that only those who could profess belief are the proper subjects for baptism. These new radical groups began to form communities and spread throughout Germany.

Melanchthon wrote to Luther expressing great distress over these radicalized groups, using the analogy of a dam breaking to describe what was going on. He wanted Luther to come home and address these issues. The town council also desired to have Luther back, and they issued a formal invitation to him to return to Wittenberg. Luther was resolved to accept this invitation and to make a public return to his home, even though he knew by doing so he was risking his own life.

The Return to Wittenberg

In March of 1522, Luther made his return to his adopted hometown. He was eager to solicit the help of fellow scholars as he was struggling with completing his translation of the Old Testament from its original Hebrew. He was also eager to assist his colleagues with stemming some of the chaos resulting from the Radical Reformers. But his return visit to Wittenberg was not filled with unmitigated joy and anticipation. Luther knew full well that he would no longer be hidden in the defensible castle in Wartburg. Luther was returning to public life, and this meant he was placing himself at personal risk.

Upon returning to Wittenberg, Luther commenced efforts to quell some of the more radical practices that had emerged in his absence. He attempted to rein in the extremists by condemning the practices of rioting and of demolishing church property. Luther believed such radical behavior was actually assisting Rome rather than harming it. His efforts met with some success, and many of the Radical Reformers fell back into line, including his old friend Karlstadt. Luther was restoring order and giving direction to the movement he founded.

The return to Wittenberg also marked a pivot point in Luther's life and work. He was transitioning into a much more calculated and diplomatic consolidator of the Reformation. While he did not abandon his attacks on Rome, his time was spent mainly in articulating the doctrine for the new church that was emerging from the upheaval of the Reformation. Luther and his views were maturing, and he took seriously his new roles and responsibilities. He was becoming a leader as well as a Reformer.

Chapter 8

Leader, Husband, and Theologian

After returning to Wittenberg in 1522, Luther settled into his new role as leader of the German Reformation. His life had become more complex and his decisions more important. He attempted to keep the young Reformation on track but still had periodic struggles with the Radical Reformers. This struggle would erupt in a profound way in 1525.

The Peasants' War

Martin Luther was a hero to the people of Germany, particularly those with the least amount of influence. He symbolized the reality that one man could stand in the face of great power and wealth and succeed in challenging it, and he gave hope to all those who felt oppressed. His actions had not only religious ramifications but political ones as well.

Most people in Germany during Luther's time were peasants who were subsistence farmers or tradesmen serving the nobility of Germany. They were often mistreated and suffered at the hands of the nobles, and this often led to sporadic uprisings on the part of the peasants. One such uprising occurred in 1525, and Luther found himself right in the thick of it.

The Peasants' War of 1525 was caused by a variety of factors, the primary one being the efforts of the German nobles to extract higher fees from the peasants. They did this by raising rents on their land, charging for rights to water, and instituting fees for hunting and fishing their lands. This did not go over well with the peasants who worked the lands of the nobles. Tensions were rising, and conflict seemed inevitable.

Luther responded as a statesman. He expressed sympathy for the peasants, urged peace, and encouraged negotiations between the conflicting parties. He wrote tracts on the subject, but by the time they were published it was too late. The peasants had already taken up arms against the nobles, and the uprising spread rapidly across the countryside of Germany. Things were quickly getting out of hand.

After witnessing firsthand the peasant uprising and the chaos that was emerging around him, Luther eventually changed the tone and substance of his response. After trying to quell the chaos and encourage the peasants to pursue a more constructive course, he shifted to taking a very harsh stance against them. He saw their rebellious actions as a threat to order and peace and eventually endorsed the efforts of the nobles to suppress the rebellion by any means necessary, including violence. He issued a tract titled *Against the Murdering and Thieving Hordes of the Peasants*. The nobles followed Luther's counsel and crushed the peasant revolt with great severity. Approximately one hundred thousand peasants were slain across Germany. It was a bloodbath.

In the aftermath of the violent crackdown on the peasants, Luther consolidated his thought on the issue. He continued holding the position that the nobles were justified in crushing the rebellion by necessary force and violence, but he criticized some of the extreme brutality that was exercised by the nobles in their response to the uprising. Luther was a man who held disdain for disorder. Ultimately, this placed him on the side of the nobles, and his writings served to entrench their power over the peasants.

Luther is frequently criticized by historians for his actions and responses related to the Peasants' War. There is little doubt that his early writings and sympathetic comments encouraged the peasants to revolt. There is equally little doubt that his later writings and condemnations of the peasants played into the hands of the nobles and provided them with justification for their excessively violent response. What is less clear is whether Luther could have stopped any of this. The issues involved in the Peasants' War were broad and primarily economic and political in nature. It was really beyond the scope of Luther's expertise and the sphere of his power. While he may not have been able to stop the forces that led to the Peasants' War and the brutal response of the nobles, his divergent comments and wavering on the issue certainly made the situation worse. In the end, one can see Luther's choice as simply a self-interested one of selecting the nobility over the people, but that would be an oversimplification. While this was clearly not Luther's brightest moment, his real choice in the Peasants' War was that of order over chaos.

Keeping the Radical Reformers in check and dealing with peasant uprisings definitely weighed heavy on Luther. He was now managing the chaos that had erupted as a result of the Reformation he started. His challenges were new and profound. But Luther did not have to face these challenges alone. He soon gained a very important personal ally.

Luther Takes a Wife

Luther had long advocated that the clergy marry. He even wrote on the topic in *The Estate of Marriage*. However, Luther himself had yet to take a wife. That changed in June of 1525, the same year as the Peasants' War, when Luther married a former nun named Katharina von Bora, whom he affectionately called Katie, sometimes even referring to her as Lord Katie!

Katharina von Bora entered a convent at the age of ten. Her father chose to leave her there, and she grew accustomed to the convent, eventually taking her vows to become a nun at the age of sixteen. In the early 1520s, when Luther's writings were well circulated and becoming increasingly popular, Katie decided that she wished to leave both the convent and her vows. Such a move was very risky because unmarried women did not have many options at this time. Katie, however, was not timid. She was a bold, strong, and independent-minded woman, and she was ready and willing to venture out on her own.

In 1523, she and some of her fellow nuns contacted Luther, seeking his aid. The nuns eventually concocted an amazing escape plan whereby they were smuggled out of the convent in pickle barrels! After escaping the convent, the nuns made their way to Wittenberg, the center of this new liberation movement.

Luther took responsibility for the nuns upon their arrival in Wittenberg and sought to find them suitable homes and husbands. Some of Luther's colleagues suggested that he could solve the predicament for one of these ex-nuns by taking one as a wife for himself. Luther balked at this suggestion. It was not that he lacked interest in having a wife but rather that he still expected to be executed for his views. While he desired a wife, he was not interested in making her an instant widow.

Luther eventually arranged for the marriages of eight of the nine nuns. The only one remaining was Katie. It was now 1525, and she had been seeking a husband for nearly two years. She was laboring in domestic service as she awaited a solution to her problem. Luther made several attempts to arrange a marriage for Katie, but each attempt met with failure. Katie, who was twenty-six years old at the time, faced the risk of becoming a spinster.

Eventually, Luther was persuaded to marry Katie, and they were wed in June of 1525. Luther saw his action as solving Katie's problem and justifying the many things he had written about clergy marrying. In essence, he desired to practice what he had preached and to lead by example. But his marriage to Katie was not just a calculated move; Luther had genuine affection for his new wife.

Luther was forty-two years old when he married. He was a long-time bachelor, and Katie quickly brought order to the chaos of Luther's domestic life. Luther even mentioned that before Katie came along he made his bed but once a year. He had many quips about Katie and the experiences of their marriage. He laughingly remarked about waking up to find her pigtails on his pillow.

Katie soon became a trusted friend and counselor to Luther. She often chastised and challenged him, thus earning the title that Luther bestowed

on her—Lord Katie. She particularly challenged
Luther during his bouts with depression. She once
took the door of his study because of his penchant
for locking himself in there in order to brood.

Both took well to their new responsibilities
as husband and wife. Luther actually focused on
earning money to support his wife. He never really
received any compensation for his books, but he
did receive a stipend from the university. Katie
focused on domestic matters and showed great
thrift in managing the home. Although they were
not rich, they were happy. After their first year
together, Luther noted how pleased he was with his
choice to marry.

Soon after their marriage, Martin and Katie
embarked on another adventure as Katie became
pregnant in October of 1525. In June of 1526, Katie
gave birth to a son, Hans. Over the succeeding
eight years, five more children followed: three girls
and two boys.

Katie also handled a great deal of hospitality.
Luther was a celebrity, and his table was rarely
empty. In fact, the Luther home often welcomed
Melanchthon and the young students from Wittenberg. They would gather around the table in

the Luther home and enjoy food and conversation. Katie provided the food and drink, and Martin provided the quips and quotes. The times around the Luthers' table were special, and Luther was very free and relaxed in his home. He would respond to the quick succession of questions from his students. They in turn wrote down many of Luther's responses, assembled them, and published them as *Table Talk*. These informal comments provided great insight into Luther and his thought. Katie contributed to creating a warm environment in which Luther could let down his guard and enjoy the company of his comrades.

While there was much joy and revelry in the Luther home, it unfortunately also had its share of trials and tragedy. The Luthers lost their daughter Elizabeth during her first year. The most poignant loss they experienced was the death of their daughter Magdalena at the age of fourteen. Luther held her in his arms as she died. Her death, understandably, crushed both him and Katie.

Overall, Martin and Katie had a joyous, passionate, and happy marriage. Luther embraced marriage as he did other aspects of his life—with boldness and conviction. Katie was a perfect mate for him, and their marriage also served as a model for other clergy. Through his marriage to Katie, Luther lived what he taught.

The Bondage of the Will

Desiderius Erasmus Roterodamus (1466–1536), or as he is most often referred to, Erasmus of Rotterdam, was one of the leading intellectuals and scholars during the late fifteenth and early sixteenth centuries. He also emerged as one of Luther's most formidable intellectual opponents. Erasmus was not wholly opposed to the critique of the church offered by Luther. He too wrote critically of the Church of Rome at times. But while Erasmus shared some sympathies with Luther regarding the state of the Church of Rome, he did not agree with Luther's methods and many of his theological conclusions. Erasmus remained a loyal Roman Catholic his entire life.

One of the major theological disputes that arose between Erasmus and Luther was over the issue of free will and predestination. Erasmus contended that God had provided mankind with free will, that humans have the capacity to choose good or evil. For Erasmus, the reality of free will was necessary to prove the justice of God in condemning those who freely choose to reject God and is required to make baptism and repentance meaningful acts. Erasmus argued that God's grace worked in tandem with human free will. In 1524, he put his views in writing in a work titled *On the Freedom of the Will*, which was a direct assault on Luther's teachings.

Luther was never one to sit idly by or to shrink from a challenge. After the publication of *On the Freedom of the Will*, Luther set to work on a response. In 1525, Luther published one of his most famous and lasting works, *On the Bondage of the Will*. In this work, Luther set forth his views on sin and its impact on human nature. He argued that original sin had so incapacitated the human condition, including the exercise of the will, humanity was incapable of coming to know God in the absence of the bestowal of God's grace. In other words, Luther did not see human will and God's grace as cooperating with one another. For Luther, God had to overcome the will of man by His grace.

For Luther, the matter of the will was an issue that had profound implications for how we understand ourselves and God. By emphasizing the exclusive work of God in salvation, Luther made it clear that God was sovereign over this process. Salvation is *sola gratia*—by grace alone. Luther also argued that the understanding of the relationship between God's will and human will he was advocating resulted in maximizing the glory of God. Luther believed Erasmus's view placed the glory in man. Salvation, according to Luther, was not only by grace alone but also *soli Deo gloria*—for the glory of God alone.

Luther's critique of Erasmus's thought did sometimes veer into personal assaults. He often displayed a level of arrogance and disdain for Erasmus, and Melanchthon often despaired over Luther's harsh treatment of his rival. As with many theological debates, the issues became muddied by personal friction. Frankly, Luther did not care for Erasmus, and the two men could not be more different. Luther was self-assured and, at times, pugnacious. Erasmus was a quiet intellectual, reserved in his speech and writings. Luther was a bold rebel and Erasmus was a reserved scholar.

Even with its faults and occasionally acerbic nature, Luther's exchange with Erasmus on the topic of the will of man remains of great use to the church. These two towering intellects put a fine point on a debate that continues within the church and is fundamental to understanding the nature of salvation. *The Bondage of the Will* is perhaps the greatest written contribution made by Martin Luther, and its relevance continues because the issues it addresses are of the utmost significance to the essence of the gospel.

A Summary of the Early Years (1522–1525)

The early years after Luther's return to Wittenberg reveal a maturing Luther in several ways. He was challenged by the excesses of the Radical Reformers, but he learned about diplomacy, compromise, and how to capably administer a newly forming church. The tragedy of the Peasants' War was humbling to Luther, and he learned how dangerous politics can be. He learned from this very difficult experience. His marriage to Katie rounded out his life. He was now a husband and a father. He had a home and a partner who would encourage and challenge him. Not only was he growing as a leader of the Reformation and his home, he also continued to develop his intellectual gifts during this time by engaging in what is perhaps his most skilled theological debate as he sparred with the renowned Erasmus over the will of man and the sovereignty of God. During these early years of the Reformation, Luther became a leader, a husband, and a refined intellectual theologian. These are all skills that Luther would soon need as he was emerging as a leader of something entirely new—an organized church that was not under the authority of a pope.

Chapter 9
A Church Is Born

The early years after Luther's return to Wittenberg were chaotic. He was preoccupied with the challenges of the Radical Reformers and the turmoil of the Peasants' War. After 1525, he was able to settle into his role as the leader of the German Reformation. His theology continued to mature, and the movement he started was consolidating into a new church.

Whether Luther intended it or not, he was becoming the founder of a distinct and separate church. The Reformation was spreading throughout continental Europe, and in each place it blossomed it had its own distinct leader and flavor. The pope and the church at Rome were no longer Luther's main foe; instead, Luther found himself in disputes and debates with other Protestant Reformers. This process forced Luther to further refine his views in relation to other Reformers. The result was that he was defining what would become the Lutheran Church.

The Liturgy and Music of the Church

It is very easy to forget that despite Luther's disagreements with Rome, he was steeped in the liturgy of the Roman Catholic Church. Luther had initially focused all his efforts on matters of salvation and the authority of the Bible. He really had not given much thought to the area of liturgy and church music. As Luther and his Reformation matured, he began to realize that the area of liturgy and church music required reformation as well.

Luther's first step in reforming the liturgy of the church involved his revision of the traditional Latin Mass into a new German version. The changes were not just in language. Luther's German liturgy removed the sacrificial emphases that were present in the Latin Mass. The celebration of the Eucharist would no longer be seen by the church as a sacrifice of the actual body and blood of Jesus. Luther also emphasized singing in his liturgical reforms. Prior to the Reformation, the church did not have a substantial body of hymns as we do today. Luther changed this. Arguably, his alterations to the music of the church may well be his most radical change to the worship of the church. Luther had great affection for music and was a moderately skilled musician. He played the lute and enjoyed singing. He had sufficient musical skills to write hymns and even to arrange the music for them. Luther was also able to encourage and inspire others to take up the task of glorifying God through music. Luther's love of song was contagious, and he fostered the growth of hymnody. He once noted that music was only second to theology in importance to the life of the Christian and the church.

The most radical of these musical reforms was perhaps Luther's effort to expand the role of the congregation in singing. Historically, only the priest and the choir would sing; the congregants were mostly passive when it came to church music, but Luther made it a participatory exercise. It must have been an amazing thing for the members of these congregations to finally lift up their voices in praise to their God. Luther was passionate about this reform and saw it as a significant part of his doctrine of the priesthood of all believers. He maintained that the laity should have the

Scriptures preached in their vernacular and a song of praise on their lips.

The introduction of congregational hymn singing was such a radical and revolutionary event that the people were in many ways unprepared for it. In other words, they were not very good at singing. They simply had no practice or experience. Everything was new. Luther recognized that training was needed to adapt to this practice. Accordingly, he organized midweek training sessions to teach the laity to sing, and singing in the home was encouraged. Reports from this period note that the singing of hymns could be heard on the streets as people reveled in this new freedom to praise God in their own language.

Luther's reforms to the music of the church included the publication of a hymnbook. The earliest of Luther's hymnbooks was published in 1524 and contained a mere twenty-three hymns. Later editions expanded the number of hymns, including Luther's most famous hymn, "A Mighty Fortress Is Our God." Luther based this hymn on the text of Psalm 46, and it profoundly captures the spirit of the Reformation and the internal psychological mind-set of Luther himself.

Luther also understood the power of music to teach the trust of the Scriptures. We moderns all know the power of a good advertising jingle that sticks in our head whether we desire it or not. Luther grasped that music was not only celebratory but educational in nature. It could be used to teach. Consider, for example, how Luther used his hymn "Our Father, Thou in Heaven Above" to teach the Lord's Prayer:

> Our Father, Thou in heaven above,
> Who biddest us to dwell in love,
> As brethren of one family,
> To cry in every need to Thee,
> Teach us no thoughtless word to say,
> But from our inmost heart to pray.
>
> Thy name be hallowed. Help us, Lord,
> In purity to keep Thy Word,
> That to the glory of Thy name
> We walk before Thee free from blame.
> Let no false doctrine us pervert;
> All poor, deluded souls convert.
>
> Thy kingdom come. Thine let it be
> In time and in eternity.
> Let Thy good Spirit e'er be nigh

Our hearts with graces to supply.
Break Satan's power, defeat his rage;
Preserve Thy Church from age to age.

Thy gracious will on earth be done
As 'tis in heaven before Thy throne;
Obedience in our weal and woe
And patience in all grief bestow.
Curb flesh and blood and every ill
That sets itself against Thy will.

Give us this day our daily bread
And let us all be clothed and fed.
From war and strife be our Defense,
From famine and from pestilence,
That we may live in godly peace,
Free from all care and avarice.

Forgive our sins, Lord, we implore,
Remove from us their burden sore,
As we their trespasses forgive
Who by offenses us do grieve.
Thus let us dwell in charity
And serve our brother willingly.

Into temptation lead us not.
When evil foes against us plot
And vex our souls on every hand,
Oh, give us strength that we may stand

Firm in the faith, a well-armed host,
Through comfort of the Holy Ghost!

From evil, Lord, deliver us;
The times and days are perilous.
Redeem us from eternal death,
And when we yield our dying breath,
Console us, grant us calm release,
And take our souls to Thee in peace.

Amen, that is, So shall it be.
Confirm our faith and hope in Thee
That we may doubt not, but believe
What here we ask we shall receive.
Thus in Thy name and at Thy word
We say: Amen. Oh, hear us, Lord! Amen.

In a pre-literate world, a hymn like this could have profound pedagogical value in teaching people the Lord's Prayer. Luther understood that music and hymns would put the words of the Bible on the lips of the people.

Luther also understood the power of music to lift the soul of the believer. He understood depression, gloom, and melancholy because he suffered from these ailments of the mind and soul. He personally found solace in music and believed this power of music would be of benefit to the entire church. Luther made the following comment regarding the power of music:

> Music is one of the best arts; the notes give life to the text; it expels melancholy, as we see in king Saul. Kings and princes ought to maintain music, for great potentates and rulers should protect good and liberal arts and laws; though private people have desire thereunto and love it, yet their ability is not adequate. We read in the Bible, that the good and godly kings maintained and paid singers. Music is the best solace for a sad and sorrowful mind; by it the heart is refreshed and settled again in peace.[1]

While Luther saw music as a gift to the church and an area requiring reform and renewal, other Reformers did not share the same view. For example, the Swiss Reformer Ulrich Zwingli (1484–1531) vehemently disagreed with Luther on the area of music. He maintained that instrumental music was an inappropriate medium for worship and called for it to be removed entirely from the liturgy of the

---

1. Martin Luther, *Table Talk*, Christian Classics Ethereal Library, http://www.ccel.org/ccel/luther/tabletalk.

church. Zwingli based his views on the connection of musical instruments to Old Testament temple worship and the utter silence of the New Testament (other than symbolic imagery in the book of Revelation) in sanctioning the use of instruments in the worship of the church. This was not the only debate that Luther would have with Zwingli and other Reformers.

The Sacraments of the Church: The Marburg Colloquy

Another area of sparring between Luther and other Protestant Reformers was over the understanding of Christ's presence in the Lord's Supper. While Luther's liturgy put the bread and cup in the hands of the laity for the first time and removed the sacrificial emphasis from the Mass, Luther still maintained the physical presence of Christ in the celebration of the Lord's Supper. He could not get past the Latin phrase *hoc est corpus meum*—"This is My body." For Luther, Jesus had stated in the Scripture that the bread of the supper was His body, and he was not willing to entertain a completely spiritualized or symbolic understanding of this declaration. This frustrated his fellow Continental

Reformers, who felt that Luther was too close to the Roman Catholic understanding of the Lord's Supper. They were pushing him to reconsider his views. Luther never liked to be pushed.

His understanding of Christ's presence in the Lord's Supper is difficult to grasp. It is best understood by contrasting it with the other two major views. First, there is the view of the Roman Catholic Church, which maintains that the bread and wine, by means of the sacramental act, experience a change in substance and become the actual body and blood of Christ. This view is known as transubstantiation, and Luther vehemently disagreed with it. The second view was that of the other Continental Reformers led, most notably, by Ulrich Zwingli. This view, in its most extreme form, maintained that the elements of the Lord's Supper were merely symbolic and represented only a memorial and reminder of Christ's completed work. For Zwingli, Christ's true presence could be in only one place—heaven. This view is often referred to as the memorial or symbolic view. Luther also vigorously opposed Zwingli's symbolic view of the Lord's Supper.

Luther agreed with Zwingli that the bread and wine were not changed into the substance of

Christ's body and blood, but he disagreed with
Zwingli regarding his view of the presence of
Christ. Luther believed that Christ's physical body
shared the divine attribute of omnipresence, so
that Christ could be physically located with the
Father in heaven while still having a true presence
in the Lord's Supper. While the bread and wine did
not change into Christ's body and blood, Luther
contended that Christ was physically present in,
with, and under the elements—that Christ's physical body became sacramentally united with the
elements. Luther's view is often referred to as con-
substantiation, although he preferred speaking of
his view as sacramental union.

In October of 1529, this disagreement between
Luther and Zwingli over the Lord's Supper came to
a head. In an effort to resolve the friction between
these two Reformers, a meeting was organized to
dispute the matter at a castle in Marburg, Germany. While a group of Reformers had gathered,
the two main players were Luther and Zwingli.
They proceeded to engage in a lively disputation
over the proper understanding of the Lord's Supper. The debates became quite heated at times, and
the two men exchanged personal attacks. Luther

even accused Zwingli of being a heretic! Although
the two men eventually tempered their comments
and became more cordial toward each other, no
agreement was reached. Neither side would budge
on the issue, and after three days they went their
separate ways.

The nuances of Luther's view on the Lord's Supper are hard to grasp and can seem esoteric. It is
much easier to understand the Roman Catholic
and Zwinglian views. Perhaps Luther simply could
not fully escape his own past and reverence for the
Mass. As you will recall, he nearly had a nervous
breakdown the first time he, as a priest, officiated
over the Mass. But perhaps the best way of understanding Luther's tenacity in maintaining a view
of the Lord's Supper that incorporates the reality
of Christ's physical presence is his view of Scripture. Luther believed that Scripture was the final
authority, and he could not get past Christ's own
declaration, "This is My body."

The Doctrine and Education of the Church

As the Reformation continued to spread throughout Europe, the pressure increased to define the
beliefs of this burgeoning movement. The rapid

growth of the Reformation did produce some chaos. Factions were emerging. The political leaders desired to see this new movement consolidated, unified, and defined. It is difficult to understand this desire in our modern age in which most Western democratic governments have distanced themselves from any connection to religion. In Luther's day, it was the exact opposite. The state was intimately involved in the affairs of the church and desired to control the church. This attempt to exercise control over the church would lead to a significant struggle between church and state in the next century as the Reformation blossomed in England and Scotland. For now, however, no one debated the state's involvement and interest in the affairs of the church.

The Augsburg Confession

The first major effort to consolidate and define the views of the Reformation church was initiated by Charles V, the Holy Roman emperor. In January 1530, Charles V summoned another diet to meet in Augsburg, Germany. Luther and the Wittenberg Reformers did not totally trust Charles V—after all, he was not exactly friendly to Luther's cause at the Diet of Worms. They cautiously accepted the call to be part of this new diet and prepared a written summation of their views. When it came time to attend the diet in person in May of 1530, the Wittenberg group decided that Luther should not attend, in order to keep him safe. This left most of the heavy lifting for Philip Melanchthon, and he was well suited for the job. Melanchthon was much more reserved than Luther. He was contemplative and more inclined to recognize the legitimacy of the papacy and the Church of Rome. He was also an excellent scholar and would prove invaluable in articulating the theology of Wittenberg. Luther, however, feared that his colleague would compromise too much.

In the end, the Diet of Augsburg yielded the Augsburg Confession (1530). The confession included twenty-eight separate articles setting forth the faith of the Reformation church. It was unapologetically representative of the Lutheran Reformation. Melanchthon would later provide significant editorial improvements to the document and also additional supportive argumentation for its positions. The document was highly regarded and represented the first real attempt to consolidate and articulate the theology of the Reformation. It would serve as a basis for future confessional statements produced by other Reformers and Reformation churches. It almost achieved a true consolidation of the various factions of the Reformation, but ultimately it was unable to contain these disparate movements under one umbrella. Today, the document represents the foundation of modern Lutheranism.

Clearly, Melanchthon deserves most of the credit for the Augsburg Confession, but there would be no Melanchthon nor an Augsburg Confession without Luther. While Luther's pen was not put to the paper of the confession, his thought and spirit resound from its contents.

While Luther was a distant participant at Augsburg, he was intimately involved in other efforts to train the new church in the area of doctrine. He continued to translate both the Old and New Testaments so that the Bible would be available to the laity in its own tongue. While Luther's translations were not without faults, his efforts proved invaluable to the needs of the growing Lutheran Church.

The Large and Small Catechisms

Luther was also concerned with providing theological instruction to the laity, and thus, in 1529, he undertook the task of preparing catechisms for the church: a large catechism for the adults and a small catechism for the children, which he envisioned as being used in the home by fathers to train their children in the nurture and admonition of the Lord. He saw his catechisms as providing structure and support to the preaching of the gospel. The small catechism, focused on children, shows an amazing level of care and thoughtfulness for young minds. Luther understood how to reach children, and he counted his catechisms among his most significant and beloved works.

Public Education

Luther viewed education as an essential element of building the church. While the two catechisms he authored would help families to grow in the Lord, Luther believed that formal public education of children was vital to the future health of the church. In 1530 he made his views public in his sermon titled "Sermon on Keeping Children in School."

Luther believed that public education was necessary so that the laity could embrace and hold fast to the truths of the Scriptures. He also believed that public education was essential to producing an educated clergy. Accordingly, Luther advocated that all boys, regardless of their apparent intellectual abilities, be educated.

Luther's efforts to produce an educated laity and a skilled clergy would have broad societal implications. This was really the beginning of the idea of broad-based public education, and it all started with Luther's desire to see the church built and sustained.

Refuting False Teaching

Another component of Luther's efforts to teach the church was his vigorous efforts to combat what he viewed as false teachings. The Anabaptists were Luther's main concern and primary target. He had wrestled with the Anabaptists, or Radical Reformers, before, but he rekindled his efforts in 1532 with the publication of his letter titled *On Infiltrating and Clandestine Preachers*. This letter, which was addressed to the growing Reformation church, contained a warning against embracing the errors of the Anabaptists. Luther particularly attacked the Anabaptist position that infants should not be baptized. He disdained their belief that the only proper subjects of baptism were adult confessing believers and their practice of rebaptizing adults who had been baptized as infants. Luther called on the church, particularly those in authority, to protect the simple from these false teachings. He saw this as an act of pastoral protection. Whether Luther was justified in his views regarding the Anabaptists, there is no doubt that he saw them and their teachings as the greatest threat to the life of the young church he sought to nurture and protect.

The reason Luther was so concerned with the Anabaptists was their tendency toward promoting social disorder and political anarchy. Luther viewed them as a threat to both his church and German society. His concerns were not without justification, as can be witnessed in the events that took place in what is known as the Munster Rebellion (1535), which involved an Anabaptist armed takeover of the city of Munster from its legitimate political officials. The takeover was led by charismatic preachers who claimed direct revelation from God and set themselves up as a new authority, above even the Bible itself. The results were horrific, including brutal murders and sexual perversions such as polygamy. The full accounting of what occurred during the Munster Rebellion is beyond the scope of this volume, but the events there reveal why Luther was so adamantly opposed to the Anabaptists—to Luther they were promoters of social disorder and chaos.

A Reformation Book of Proverbs

As noted earlier in the discussion of Luther's domestic life with Katie, one of the great contributions of the home they created together was the discussion that occurred around their table. It was during these informal interactions between Luther and his students that the Reformer set forth his heart and mind in an unparalleled manner. Luther wrote academic treatises and spoke before formal tribunals, but it was in the pages of *Table Talk* where we see Luther unfiltered. His students faithfully recorded his answers on a variety of topics and consolidated them under headings to make them useful. His comments were published and remain today as one of his most popular written works. There are over sixty-five hundred entries representing Luther's thoughts about issues crucial to the church. Here are just a few selections to give a flavor of this work.[2]

The Word of God

No greater mischief can happen to a Christian people, than to have God's Word taken from them, or falsified, so that they no longer have it pure and clear. God grant we and our descendants be not witnesses of such a calamity.

The Nature of the World

There are three sorts of people: the first, the common sort, who live secure without remorse of conscience, acknowledging not their corrupt manners and natures, insensible of God's wrath, against their sins, and careless thereof. The second, those who through the law are scared, feel God's anger, and strive and wrestle with despair. The third, those that acknowledge their sins and God's merited wrath, feel themselves conceived and born in sin, and therefore deserving of perdition, but, notwithstanding, attentively hearken to the gospel, and believe

---

2. Quotations from Luther's *Table Talk* can be found at http://www.ccel.org/ccel/luther/tabletalk.

that God, out of grace, for the sake of Jesus Christ, forgives sins, and so are justified before God, and afterwards show the fruits of their faith by all manner of good works.

Of Prayer

The Lord's prayer binds the people together, and knits them one to another, so that one prays for another, and together one with another; and it is so strong and powerful that it even drives away the fear of death.

Of Preachers and Preaching

I would not have preachers torment their hearers, and detain them with long and tedious preaching, for the delight of hearing vanishes therewith, and the preachers hurt themselves.

The defects in a preacher are soon spied; let a preacher be endued with ten virtues, and but one fault, yet this one will eclipse and darken all his virtues and gifts, so evil is the world in these times.

Of the Devil and His Works

He who will have, for his master and king, Jesus Christ, the son of the Virgin, who took upon himself our flesh and our blood, will have the devil for his enemy.

Of Luther's Adversaries

Erasmus of Rotterdam is the vilest miscreant that ever disgraced the earth.

Such fellows as Tetzel, Cochlaeus, Lemnius, I nothing regard. We should have no dealing with such backbiters and slanderers, they are most detestable; they appear not openly in the field, nor come right in our sight, but, in their poisoned hatred, scorn everything we do. They boast highly of the Fathers; let them; we have one Father, which is in heaven who is above all fathers; their piece and patchwork is of no weight. They write under the inspiration of a corrupt and vicious heart, and we all know that their works are mere impudent lies.

Table Talk remains a window into the heart, mind, and soul of Luther. His comments reveal his virtues, his genius, and his flaws. It also provided a useful guide to his students and other church leaders. It was a Reformation book of proverbs, wisdom for those serving in the growing Reformation church.

Teaching the Bible and Training Pastors

Finally, Luther endeavored to edify the church by means of teaching the truth of the Scriptures. Of course, he did this by means of his preaching, but he also contributed to the education of the church through his work as a professor. It has already been noted that Luther provided the church with a Bible in the German language by means of his translation efforts, but he also provided the church with a voluminous commentary and lectures on portions of the Bible.

Luther loved to teach the Scriptures. In the 1530s, he once again turned his attention to the study of the Scriptures, and he shared his lessons with the students at the University of Wittenberg. Unsurprisingly, Luther focused on the writings of the apostle Paul, particularly his letter to the Galatians. He believed that this letter contained the most poignant and clear teaching of the gospel. His lectures on Galatians took nearly three years to complete. Melanchthon and Luther's students made certain that these lectures were edited and published so that they could benefit the church.

Luther also initiated a variety of reforms at the University at Wittenberg to better enable the training and ordination of future pastors. Eventually, he invested the theological faculty at Wittenberg with the power to ordain men to the ministry in the absence of a proper bishop. Luther began to detail the qualifications he believed were necessary for a man to be a good pastor. These included the ability to teach, skills in articulation, verbal strength and eloquence, a good memory, and diligence. At Wittenberg, Luther created a Reformation seminary to serve the growing church.

From Reformation to Lutheranism

By 1530, it was clear that Luther was no longer the bombastic monk fighting the pope and the Church of Rome. He was now the leader of his own church, burdened with the responsibility of reforming liturgy, worship, and doctrine. He was becoming ever more pastoral, concerned for the care and feeding of the Lord's sheep. He was in many ways the father of this new church that would eventually bear his name.

Chapter 10
The Latter Years

As Luther entered the decade of the 1530s, he began to feel the weight of his many responsibilities. He was a father, husband, church leader, political leader, education reformer, professor, and pastor. The overwhelming burdens placed on him began to take their toll.

Physical and Mental Struggles

Luther was never a very healthy man. He seemed to be always beset with some malady. In the early 1530s, Luther began to experience more severe symptoms from his many ailments. In March of 1531, Luther's personal correspondence revealed that he felt a significant decline in his health and stamina. He complained that he was living as a "sick man" and described his deep sense of fatigue. During the early 1530s, he complained about debilitating pain in his head. Other ailments included episodes of dizziness and even an ooz-ing open sore on his leg. Luther's personal papers from this period reveal that he was convinced that he would die soon.

Depression, gloom, and melancholy also assaulted Luther during this period of his life. Often he would enter into a period of depres-sion because he doubted the goodness of God and that God loved him. The law of God always threatened Luther. Even though he had so vigor-ously defended and proclaimed the gospel, he still struggled with its application to his own life. Luther tried to make sense of his depression and to devise ways to escape its snare. He was not very successful at avoiding depression, but he did come to see in it an opportunity to grow in his faith. Luther was convinced that some of his episodes of depression were direct assaults from either God or the devil, and he sometimes engaged in heated debates with one or the other.

Luther's physical ailments worsened with age. As his life spanned into the 1540s, his body began to break down. By 1540, Luther was fifty-seven years old and had lived a hard and stressful life. He experienced severe kidney troubles, including kidney stones, which were at times quite severe. The headaches also continued and sometimes left Luther utterly incapacitated.

Luther's Errors

As Luther entered into old age he became harsher in his personal attacks against his enemies. At times, he descended into base name calling, and there was a growing bitterness in the tone of his writings. For example, his last published essay, *Against the Papacy: An Institution of the Devil*, was particularly harsh in its criticisms of the pope and the Church of Rome. Unlike Luther's earlier criticisms of Rome, which attacked the dogma, doctrine, and authority of the pope, this particular essay frequently devolved into mere crass name calling. Luther referred to the pope in ways that would offend the sensibilities of most modern Christians, including to referring to the pope in "donkey-like" terminology and making frequent references to the pope and flatulence. This essay was published in 1545, just one year before Luther's death.

During the 1540s, Luther also wrote about Jews living in Germany. He published three essays on the topic, with the most prominent and well-known one being *On the Jews and Their Lies* (1543). In this treatise, Luther advocated a variety of radical positions, such as setting fire to Jewish homes and synagogues, taking their wealth and property, destroying elements of Judaism (the Talmud and Jewish prayer books), and forbidding Jewish rabbis from teaching the Jewish faith. In his early years, Luther had written favorable things regarding Jews and how they should be treated by Christians, but near the end of this life his tone and statements regarding Jews took a very dark turn. It was comments like these that led famed Luther biographer Roland Bainton to declare that he wished Luther would have died before being able to pen such words.

Many Lutheran biographers have attempted to explain away Luther's words regarding the Jews. It is certainly true, as noted previously, that in his early life he was supportive of Jews. It is also true that his comments on this subject are often viewed through the lens of our modern, post-Holocaust world. Some of Luther's defenders cry foul when people attempt to analyze him through this lens, believing it to be unfair because these hideous events had not occurred in Luther's time. It is also true that Luther's harsh comments regarding Jews were often fueled not by ethnic or racial hatred but rather by what Luther viewed as theological perversion and doctrinal error. When Luther thought and spoke of Jews, he was often referring to Paul's opponents at Galatia who were preaching a different gospel, a gospel of self-righteousness versus Christ's righteousness.

While all of these counterpoints with regard to Luther's comments have some merit, it is ultimately impossible to offer a defense for Luther's views on this subject and the consequences they helped to create. His writings regarding Jews were used and trumpeted by the Nazis in defense of their bigotry against Jews. Although he may not have intended it, Luther contributed to a legacy of anti-Semitism, and for that we should offer no defense or excuse for the man or his words. Instead, we should rightly criticize and denounce this aspect of his life, thought, and writings. I, like Bainton, also wish that Luther had died before being able to write these words, but Luther did write them, and for that he should be properly judged by history. It is not surprising that some modern Lutheran organizations have offered formal apologies for the writings of Luther on this subject.[1]

Although much less grave and disturbing than his writings regarding Jews, Luther also displayed regrettable and questionable behavior in his response to the well-known bigamy of Philip of Hesse (1504–1567). Also known as Philip I, landgrave of Hesse, he rose to the role of regent of Hesse (part of Germany) after his father died when he was just five years old. At the age of seventeen, Philip met Luther at the Diet of Worms. He was captivated by Luther's personality, and, at the age of twenty-four, he embraced the cause of the Reformation, primarily due to the tutelage of Melanchthon. Philip became a powerful advocate for the Reformation of the church in Germany and a trusted ally of Luther.

At the age of nineteen, Philip had an arranged marriage to Christine of Saxony, the daughter of the Duke of George. Christine was not well and was

---

1. For a detailed discussion of whether Luther should be viewed as anti-Semitic, see Eric W. Gritsch's article in *Christian History* magazine, "Was Luther Anti-Semitic?," available at http://www.christianitytoday.com/history/issues/issue-39/was-luther-anti-semitic.html.

a heavy drinker. Philip had little affection for her. Their marriage was, like many royal marriages at the time, arranged for purposes of political expediency. Philip began to share his affections elsewhere, becoming romantically involved with another woman, Margarethe von der Saale. He desired to divorce Christine, but divorce was allowed only in cases of adultery. Philip then attempted to justify his behavior by arguing the case for bigamy, citing the Old Testament patriarchs and the case of Henry VIII as examples. He noted it was better to have two wives than to divorce. Like Henry VIII, Philip attempted to get a religious stamp of approval on his behavior, and he looked to his favorite theologians, Martin Bucer, Philip Melanchthon, and Martin Luther. Bucer and Melanchthon both deferred to Luther in the matter.

Luther was unwilling to sanction divorce for Philip, but he was persuaded to accept the argument for bigamy from the Old Testament example of the patriarchs. He essentially sanctioned Philip's bigamy but counseled him to keep the matter secret because it violated the law of the state. Philip and Margarethe were married in secret on March 4, 1540, based on Luther's private sanction. Philip's sister eventually exposed him and his bigamous marriage. A scandal erupted that reflected poorly on Luther. It tarnished his reputation and also impacted Bucer and Melanchthon. Melanchthon was particularly remorseful regarding his role in this tawdry affair, and he became severely distraught and depressed as a consequence. Luther attempted to use the confessional as a fig leaf to cover his role in the matter. He claimed he had to keep everything a secret because Philip shared it with him in a private confession. Clearly, this was not one of Luther's better moments.

Luther's latter years represented a clear decline and darkening of his personality. His writings became bitter, crass, and, with regard to Jews, bigoted. Perhaps part of this can be attributed to the aging process and a decline in Luther's faculties. He did suffer many physical ailments throughout his life, which took their toll on him. He also suffered from mental stress and severe depression at times. Whatever the cause, the end of Luther's life is his least admirable period, and there is no way to soften the picture if one is attempting to portray the man as he was. Like many of the great figures of the Bible itself, Luther was a flawed man, and those flaws became more pronounced as he approached his death.

The Death of Martin Luther

In the winter of 1546, Luther was drawn back to Eisleben, the city of his birth, by family business. After Luther had decided to pursue the vocation of a monk, his brother became the heir apparent to the family copper business. The local officials were attempting to levy greater taxes on the business, and a dispute arose. Luther, against the protests of his wife, ventured home, determined to lend a hand in resolving the matter.

As already noted, Luther was not a healthy man. He did not travel well, and the German winters were not easy for him. But despite these obstacles, Luther arrived safely at Eisleben and entered into negotiations, which became protracted. On the evening of February 17, 1546, Luther suffered a heart attack. He was attended to by physicians and was able to get to bed that evening but awoke again around 1:00 a.m. the next morning due to the onset of severe chest pain. Efforts were made to revive him, but to no avail. Martin Luther died at around 3:00 a.m. on February 18, 1546.

Funeral services were held for Luther in Eisleben over a two-day period. His body was then moved to Wittenberg, where another funeral service was held. Melanchthon gave the eulogy, and in it he ranked Luther among the patriarchs and prophets of the Bible. While addressing Luther's students, Melanchthon applied to Luther the words spoken of the Old Testament prophet Elijah: "Gone is the charioteer of Israel!" Luther the man was indeed gone, but his legacy lives on.

Interestingly, soon after his death it appeared as if his legacy would come to a swift end. Charles V, the Holy Roman emperor, mustered troops for the purpose of crushing the rebellious Lutheran areas of Germany and bringing them back under his subjection. Charles had commenced what became known as the Schmalkaldic War. In 1547, Charles's troops marched into Wittenberg and took control of the city, including Luther's land. He also issued an edict requiring the return of Protestants to the Catholic Church. It appeared, for the moment, that Luther's Reformation was nearing an end.

But Charles's victory did not last. Luther's teachings and the support for the Protestant Reformation were now too firmly entrenched into German life